BLENDED FAMILIES

PREMARITAL EDITION

ANATOMY OF A BLENDED FAMILY

Drs. Larry and Carol Snapp

authorHOUSE

AuthorHouse™
1663 Liberty Drive
Bloomington, IN 47403
www.authorhouse.com
Phone: 833-262-8899

Published by AuthorHouse 01/28/2025

ISBN: 979-8-8230-4160-7 (sc)
ISBN: 979-8-8230-4159-1 (e)

Library of Congress Control Number: 2025900684

CONTENTS

ACKNOWLEDGEMENTS

First and foremost, we would like to thank God for His vision and direction to develop a curriculum for blended families. With a growing number of families being the result of remarriage, there is a need for education on how best to bring "yours, mine and ours" together in a Godly way. Obviously, God hates divorce, but since we live in a fallen world, divorce is a fact of life. We pray that this curriculum will help some of those remarriages become the covenant marriages that God desires and the cycle of divorce will end.

Thank you to Pastors Tommy and Luke Barnett who consistently encouraged us to step up to the plate and reach for the next level of service for the Kingdom of God. Thanks also for providing a great church home environment for us to grow and mature in our relationship with the Lord Jesus Christ. We always look forward to the smiles and hugs we get after each service. Seeing what the Lord is doing through both of you keeps the fire alive in us to strive to find ways to do more. This curriculum is in large part do to the inspiration we have received from you both.

Thank you to Dr. Leo and Molly Godzich for all the training and mentoring we have received. Thanks to their ministry, the National Association of Marriage Enhancement (NAME), our own marriage was restored in 2003. Through their teaching we were able to learn what a Godly marriage should be.

A very special thank you goes to Pastors Arnold and Gwen Tackett for all the love, time and tears that they shared with us as they took us hand-in-hand through our own marriage trials and tribulations. Thank you for planting the seed that eventually grew into the desire to counsel others. It totally changed the course of our lives. Thanks for helping us "Get it." We will forever be joined at the heart even though we are not currently joined at the hip. The Lord definitely has a reason for the four of us coming together. It's still unfolding, but we know it's going to be awesome!

Thanks also to Dr. and Mrs. Richard Drake whose faith, guidance, support and encouragement helped us complete this project. When the four of us met at our first Phoenix University of Theology graduation there seemed to be a very special bond created. We greatly appreciate your friendship and trust and we are looking forward to discovering what kind of adventure the Lord has in store for all of us.

A big thank you to all the couples we have had the privilege to counsel over the years. You keep proving to us that the Biblical principles outlined in this study are true. When they are applied day-by-day, they work!

And finally, thank you to our own blended family – daughters Cheryl and Michelle and son, Morrill. You have been the inspiration for much of what we are now able to share with others through the Blended Families Ministry. We hope what we've learned with you over the past 30-plus years will benefit many others.

ENDORSEMENTS

"Dr. Larry and Carol Snapp, through the Blended Family ministry, have brought healing and hope to countless individuals who have re-married or are in "blended" families in our church. Their newest endeavor, *"The Anatomy of a Blended Family"*, prepares individuals *prior* to entering marriage again. This book is beneficial in helping people to understand the various challenges associated with re-marriage, preparing them for lasting second marriages, and paving the way for healthy blended families. The Snapp's ministry has greatly impacted our congregation and I encourage other churches to use this curriculum to support and develop strong blended families for the Glory of God."

Pastor Tommy Barnett
Pastor Emeritus
Dream City Church

"In today's world there have been many changes to the makeup of the family. Here at Dream City Church we see more and more Blended Families all the time.

When Dr. Larry & Carol Snapp approached us about writing and teaching this curriculum we knew instantly that it was a ministry we here at DCC had been praying for.

Through their three books - The Blended Families Curriculum, the Leadership Manual for the instructors and now the Pre-marital Edition - churches anywhere can begin teaching it. We are very excited about this Pre-Marital guide and can't wait to begin using it. Many pastors that came to our Pastors' School this year are also very excited about this Ministry.

I recently told Larry and Carol they are gems and we are proud to have them and their Ministry at DCC. We consider Larry and Carol to be a crucial part of our leadership team here at DCC and would highly recommend that you utilize their gifting and expertise in your local body of believers."

Pastor Luke Barnett
Sr. Pastor
Dream City Church

"Being a part of a loving family is a blessing. Blended families are more common than ever before. Today, successfully blending families takes patience and a commitment from each individual, but can be very rewarding. Seventy-five percent of all divorced people eventually remarry; and I believe it is a must that these wonderful families receive answers to the challenges they face. Every church must provide ministries to the blended families in their congregation. The need is great and the answers are found with the anointed ministry of Dr. Larry and Carol Snapp. Phoenix First Assembly loves the help Larry and Carol have brought to our blended families."

Pastor Dale Lane
Executive Pastor
Dream City Church

"Everyone who has ever been married clearly understands the prayer, nurturing, effort, and attention required to flourish within it. In fact, the very best of marriages happen when both spouses unselfishly do more than their part. Many succeed and find true companionship and fulfillment, yet others unfortunately fail. In spite of our best efforts through Christian counseling and prayer for couples in crises, the divorce rate in the church now mirrors that of the world, in that nearly half of all marriages today fail. When you combine this with the premature death of a spouse, we have many single people with children looking to be married once again.

It is out of this reality that the Blended Family Ministry was created. Dr. Larry and Carol Snapp teach and counsel on blended families from their own experience of living within one for over 30 years and have been doing Biblical couples counseling for over six years. No insight is greater than when it comes from someone who has walked a mile or two in your shoes. Larry and Carol have walked those miles and are passionate about helping others to create a family environment that honors God, each other, and the entire family.

Being a part of a blended family has variety of challenges but Larry and Carol know that it is through these challenges where great success and satisfaction comes. Their experience and genuine concern for blended families and their struggles, gives us yet another opportunity to minister to people at their specific point of need. As a pastor who is responsible for teaching and guiding couples in marriage, the Snapp's ministry brings me a great sense of security, knowing their expertise will be presented with sound Biblical truth. Ultimately, we have the assurance of knowing marriages and families will be strengthened, resurrected, and saved."

Pastor David Blythe
Dream City Church

"With the growing divorce and remarriage rate in America, the need for blended family teaching in the church is a must! Drs. Larry and Carol Snapp have carefully and prayerfully comprised this excellent teaching guide based on Biblical principles and their own personal experiences. This book has been utilized to prepare and minister to many families at Phoenix First Assembly."

Pastor Shawna Lummer
Dream City Church
Director of Fusion Life Groups
Public Relations & Communications

The "Anatomy of a Blended Family" provides excellent premarital guidance for individuals faced with remarriage. In point of fact it is excellent guidance for anyone planning to marry for the first time as well. It is Christ centered, Spirit breathed counsel.

Studies have shown that less than 8% of divorced / single parents go to church regularly, because they 'don't feel the church cares about their broken lives'.

Reportedly eight out of ten pastors and church leaders in America 'don't know where to turn' for assistance on how to minister regarding step-family dynamics. As many as 87% of new blended family parents say 'we don't know where to turn to for help' for their marriage, children, step-children and new blended family.

Drs. Larry and Carol, address these challenges in a meaningful, fruitful and faithful way through their Blended Families Ministry and curriculum.

I highly recommend the curriculum and program to churches and pastors as an effective way to positively address the aforementioned serious challenges.

Dr. Richard Drake, Provost
Primus University of Theology

Dr. Larry and Carol Snapp have done an incredible job creating this wonderful premarital curriculum written specifically for the blended family. They know first-hand the joys and challenges of "blending" a family successfully. Their lives, their children and their grandchildren are a testimony of the miracle God can do when these principles are walked out. This curriculum is scripturally based with life changing truths from the Bible. We highly recommend it to couples, to churches and to pastors.

Pastors Arnold and Gwen Tackett
Victorville First Assembly-CA
Vessels of Honor

"Churches have needed a Blended Family Ministry for a long time. Dr. Larry and Carol Snapp have put together a curriculum using their 30+ years experience. I am excited about their new Pre-Marital book *"Anatomy of a Blended Family"* and how it will bless the people of PFA and around the world.

With their three curriculums in place, the 12-week course & Leadership Manual and now the Pre-Marital Book, any church can have a road map with God's guidance and will be able to help create a successful blended family."

Pastor Brad Baker
Executive Pastor
Dream City Church

FOREWORD

You've been married before and things didn't turn out so well. Perhaps you had a good relationship with your spouse, but they have been promoted to be with the Lord. Now you've gotten up the courage to try marriage again. This Pre-Marital Guide is written specifically for those of you who are ready to step out and give marriage another chance. This time, you want to get it right and do it God's Way. Included here is the wisdom gained through over 30 years of being a Blended Family and over six years of clinical experience in Biblical couple-to-couple counseling.

Unfortunately, there is usually much more time spent planning the wedding day than planning the marriage itself. This guide will give you the tools you need to be properly prepared for what happens after the wedding day. It will take you through a process to lead you to the conclusion that you are definitely ready to be married and that you are about to marry the right person – or not.

You should be 100% sure that the person you are about to marry is "the one" that God has created just for you. If, after you complete this instruction, you realize that there are red flags, DO NOT ignore them. Whatever issues those red flags represent, make sure you have dealt with them fully before the wedding. Bury all the skeletons that may be hiding in your closet so that they don't come back to haunt you. There is liberty and peace in victory. There is victory in Jesus Christ.

The preparation process will take you through the "normal" things that need to be discussed before marriage as well as the additional challenges that you are going to face due to the fact that you are about to be re-married. You will learn what challenges to expect in dealing with ex-spouses, ex-grandparents and step-children. You will learn about finances and the pressures that can be expected due to child-support and alimony payments. You will learn about the possibilities of being involved in future legal matters regarding child-support, alimony and child custody.

Marriage is serious business. Do not enter into it lightly. It requires a proper understanding of God's order for relationships and family. Without God, the additional challenges you will encounter when creating a blended family will no doubt overtake you. Marriage requires a plan. As stated in a quote attributed to Benjamin Franklin - "By failing to prepare, you are preparing to fail." By entering into marriage with the idea that, "We'll worry about that later" you are failing to prepare. In a pre-marital situation, both parties need to have their eyes open. Through counseling, the motives for the marriage need to be determined and validated that they are based in truth and honesty.

A successful marriage is built on trust. Without a foundation of truth and honesty, the marriage will be built on sand and will be easily washed away with the first small flood of trials and tribulation. This study will help you discover God's plan for marriage. Our prayer is that you will work His plan and have many years together with the one that God made just for you.

THE ANATOMY OF A BLENDED FAMILY

The anatomy of a Blended Family can be a very complicated organism. This pre-marital curriculum attempts to simplify things and give you a fighting chance at building a successful blended family where there may have been dysfunction and failure in the past.

God is not so concerned about where you have been or even where you are right now. His desire for you is an abundant life based on a very close personal relationship with His Son, Jesus Christ. He wants you to experience the blessings that come with being one of His children. This curriculum is designed with that understanding in mind.

One of the foundational scriptures for this curriculum is:

> *1 Corinthians 11:3*
> *[3] But I want you to understand that the head of every man is Christ, the head*
> *of a wife is her husband, and the head of Christ is God. (ESV)*

The diagram on the following page represents the "ideal" blended family. Everything in this book is based on using that ideal as the assumed target. It will take time and effort on your part to implement the ideas and tools described here. The expectation is not that your marriage will always be a '10', but you should be able to keep it in the '7-9' range the majority of the time. By staying in that range, you will have a very satisfying journey through life with your spouse.

Starting at the head, the diagram illustrates that a Blended Family needs to be lead by a Christ-centered husband/father. The husband (head), being the logical future looking member of the body, should receive the vision from God and set the direction for the rest of the body. The wife (neck), receiving the vision from her husband, and being the relational one, communicates the vision to the rest of the family. The diagram does not intend to imply that the neck is what turns the head. The children (hands) have to be connected to and brought under the head and neck to become part of the fully functioning blended family. Yours and mine need to become "ours". The extended family (leg), such as grandparents or aunts and uncles can be an integral part of a blended family, but there can also be situations where there will need to be boundaries. The other leg (ex-spouses) can be the one that will give you the most trouble. Like the Apostle Paul, this could quite possibly be your "thorn in the flesh".

The goal of this curriculum is to provide you with tools and the understanding to use them in order to start your blended family off on the right foot and to keep it moving in the right direction. Marriage should be a decision that is made after much prayer and with the understanding that it is a covenant. Take the vows seriously and don't be quick to bail when you end up dealing with worse instead of better or sickness instead of health. God's grace is sufficient to get you through the tough times.

THE ANATOMY DIAGRAM OF A BLENDED FAMILY

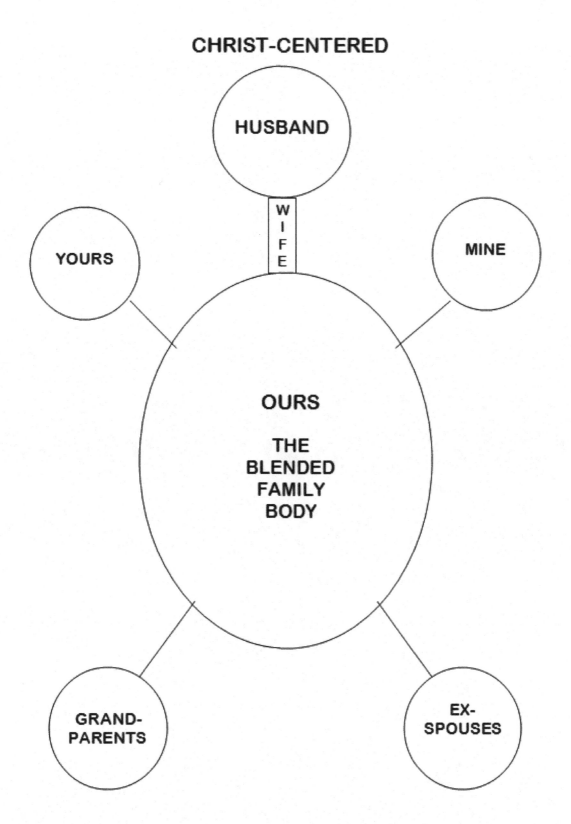

CHRIST-CENTERED — HUSBAND — WIFE — YOURS — MINE — OURS — THE BLENDED FAMILY BODY — GRAND-PARENTS — EX-SPOUSES

INTRODUCTION

This pre-marital curriculum is based on scripture taken from the King James Version of the Holy Bible. It has been written as a guide for those who plan to remarry after going through a divorce or the loss of a spouse.

The principles outlined in this study will help you learn how to put a Godly marriage together where one did not exist before. Our desire is to help you first recognize and then deal with many of the pitfalls found in marriage in general and remarriage in particular.

We will take you through Scripture and follow the road map God laid out for marriage in the beginning. We will start the study by laying the foundation for what a Godly marriage should be. From there, we will work on how to deal with the many obstacles and traps that couples often run into.

Some of the topics we will deal with include the following: baggage of past failed marriages, remarriage after divorce, remarriage after the death of a spouse, geographical, age, religious and racial cultural differences, in-law issues and step-parenting and single-parenting skills.

God has put the desire in our hearts to create this curriculum as a way to put His values back into homes and families. We are stepping out in faith based on 2nd Timothy 2:2 "And the things that thou hast heard of me among many witnesses, the same commit thou to faithful men, who shall be able to teach others also."

We hope to reach one home, one man, one woman or even one child at a time, teaching them God's plan for marriage. As they are taught, we pray they also will be able to reach other family members and friends. We also share God's vision to have this teaching spread like a virus. Only this virus won't make you sick. It will help heal you.

We hope this teaching helps you learn so you, in turn, can teach it in your home, your group or your church.

CHAPTER 1

ARE YOU REALLY READY FOR MARRIAGE?

The assumption is made here that you have been married before. You can still benefit greatly from this curriculum even if you haven't been married before, so keep reading! There is a high probability that the person you are about to marry has been previously married or has come from a family where there has been a divorce. This first section asks many questions that you need to answer prior to saying "I do".

WHY ARE YOU GETTING MARRIED NOW?

People get married for all sorts of reasons. Many of them are less desirable than others. Now is the time to be very honest with yourself. The worst person you can lie to is you. Now is the time to get wisdom and understanding as to how to get the most out of your new marriage. Another foundational scripture is Proverbs 1:5&7, *Proverbs 1:5 [5] Let the wise hear and increase in learning, and the one who understands obtain guidance, (ESV) Proverbs 1:7 [7] The fear of the LORD is the beginning of knowledge; fools despise wisdom and instruction. (ESV)*

One of the first questions that you need to answer is "Why are you getting married NOW?" Do you feel that you have fully grieved over the loss of your previous marriage or the loss of your spouse? Have you figured out the root causes that lead to the demise of the previous marriage? Have you worked on fixing those issues that were your responsibility or are you still blaming your ex-spouse for the failure? Have you forgiven your ex? Have you forgiven yourself? It's never just one person in a marriage that causes it to fail. What makes you think that this marriage will be successful? What is different about you now and what are you going to do differently than you did before?

Those are a lot of questions to answer. It should show you that marriage is something you do only after much serious consideration. A marriage is a whole lot more than a wedding. Many months often go into the planning of a wedding. The wedding is a one-day event celebrating two becoming one, but have you spent as much time planning your marriage as you have spent planning your wedding? It requires a lot of time in prayer and making sure the person with whom you are about to be joined is the one that God has created for you. You have the free will to marry any one you choose, but God has created the perfect spouse with you in mind. Choosing the wrong one short-changes you from the full blessing that God had in store for you as well as your specially created "other half".

DO YOU REALLY KNOW YOUR SPOUSE?

> *2 Corinthians 6:14*
> *The Temple of the Living God*
> *[14] Do not be unequally yoked with unbelievers. For what partnership has righteousness*
> *with lawlessness? Or what fellowship has light with darkness? (ESV)*

How well do you know the person to whom you are about to be married? How well do they know you? Have you been open with them about your past? Have they been open and honest about their past? To be successful in marriage, especially a blended family, you can't have any skeletons in your closet. They all need to be taken out and buried once and for all. If you don't, sooner or later, they will come back to haunt you.

In many cases, during the courtship period, the "real" person you are getting to know is actually the agent representing the real person. People can be on their best behavior during the dating process, even for periods of a year or more, but once you are actually married, and the deal is signed, the agent disappears and the real person finally shows up. Often, the real person you are now married to is nothing like the person that you were dating.

Ladies, do not marry with the intention of "fixing" your soon-to-be husband. Odds are unlikely that he will ever really change unless God does it from the inside out. All things are possible with God, but change only comes through the individual's relationship with Christ. The harder you try to fix him, the harder he will resist change. Men, do not expect that the woman you are about to marry will stay "just the way she is". A general rule of thumb is – "men never change – women always do".

If possible, a wise person will get to know their future in-laws very well before the wedding. Ladies, knowing your father-in-law will give you a fair idea of what your husband's tendencies will be like. Making peace with your future mother-in-law can produce many years of good will after the wedding. A future husband that is tied too tightly to his mother is a big red flag. Men, get to know your future mother-in-law. You will gain very valuable insight into what your wife will act like and eventually, look like. It will also serve you well to make the effort to find something in common with your father-in-law. Do you see the pattern here? YOU are the one that needs to make the effort that will set the tone of your in-law relationship for the years to come.

CAN YOU COMMUNICATE WITH EACH OTHER?

How well can you communicate with each other? Communication is not just talking. In actuality, it requires listening more than talking. You have two ears and one mouth. There is some significance to that. You have to be able to hear what someone is saying in order to know what it is they are trying to say. If you're just thinking about what you're going to say at the next opportunity, then you are not truly hearing what is being said. A future spouse needs to feel they are important to you and that you care about what they have to say.

Good communication is an art and requires practice. When you have developed a reasonable skill level, it helps not only reduce misunderstandings, but also allows the inevitable conflicts to be resolved in a productive manner. See *Proverbs 27:17 [17] Iron sharpens iron, and one man sharpens another. (ESV)* Sometimes when iron strikes iron, sparks fly. The long-term goal should be to learn how to have discussions that lead to conflict resolution rather than arguments about who's right and who's wrong. Make sure God's Word is your umpire. More will be presented on this in Chapter 7.

ARE YOU UP FOR THE CHALLENGES OF A BLENDED FAMILY?

A first marriage is hard enough to make work and a blended family marriage has an even higher rate of divorce than first marriages. There is very little difference between the divorce rate in "the world" and the church. In both places the divorce rate is around 50%. The divorce rate in remarriages is somewhere in the 60-70% rate and divorce generally happens more quickly than it did in the previous marriage.

If you are contemplating remarriage after a divorce or loss of a spouse, be very aware that "the odds" are against you. On the other hand, a true Christian marriage can't fail. So, there is still hope. As much as God hates divorce *(Malachi 2:16)* Satan hates marriage and wants to divide you. In preparation for entering into a blended family, you MUST be very aware that you are going to battle in spiritual warfare.

To build a successful blended family that will last a lifetime you will need to be very intentional about keeping your many relationships in God's order. A husband and a wife are to leave their father and mother and cleave to each other and become one flesh. *Genesis 2:24 [24] Therefore a man shall leave his father and his mother and hold fast to his wife, and they shall become one flesh. (ESV)*

The remaining chapters in this curriculum will take you on a journey through many of the things you will need to know to be prepared to build a successful blended family. There will be times when you will wish ex-spouses would disappear from the face of the earth. There may be legal battles over child custody/support payments or alimony. You may face many obstacles that you see as "not being fair". Life is not fair, but God is just.

You have to keep your perspective an eternal one. Keep in mind that, as a Christian, your true reward will be in Heaven and that the trials and tribulations you WILL face in your new journey are temporary and there is probably something you are supposed to learn from the experience. At the very least, it will force you to get closer to God and strengthen your relationship with Him. You are here for His purposes, not your own.

Creating a blended family will give you many opportunities to show and grow your character. God doesn't give you courage, patience or humility. He gives you opportunities to show those particular character traits. If you need more patience, He will present you with tests that will require patience in order to pass. If you have a problem with pride, He will present situations that will bring you to your knees. Marriage provides the ideal situation for God to bring you up to a higher level of spiritual maturity. You will need to have an abundance of love, grace, mercy, patience, strength, courage and humility to be successful.

EXERCISES FOR LESSON 1

1. Describe in detail your idea of the perfect date you would plan for your future spouse. Each person should write their own version without sharing.

2. Describe the relationship with your future parent-in-laws as they see you. If they are no longer living, apply the question to sibling-in-laws.

3. How well do you get along with your future step-children? If not very well, describe what <u>you</u> will do to make it better.

CHAPTER 2

UNDERSTANDING GOD'S PLAN FOR MARRIAGE

To create a successful blended family, the best place to start is establishing a solid foundation by understanding God's plan for marriage. The husband-wife relationship will be the cornerstone that the blended family is built on. The principles outlined here can be applied to any marriage, whether it's a first marriage or a remarriage. Once the foundation is set on solid ground, blended families will find the strength to weather the many situations they find themselves dealing with. In today's world, more and more families are being created out of previous marriages that have failed. In order to successfully blend multiple families together, we need to know what God intended for marriage from the beginning. Take a look at what the Scriptures reveal about the establishment of the institution of marriage. Marriage was the first institution created by God.

THE INSTITUTION OF MARRIAGE BEGINS

Genesis 1:26–28
[26] Then God said, "Let us make man in our image, after our likeness. And let them have dominion over the fish of the sea and over the birds of the heavens and over the livestock and over all the earth and over every creeping thing that creeps on the earth." [27] So God created man in his own image, in the image of God he created him; male and female he created them. [28] And God blessed them. And God said to them, "Be fruitful and multiply and fill the earth and subdue it, and have dominion over the fish of the sea and over the birds of the heavens and over every living thing that moves on the earth." (ESV)

Looking at verse 26 through 28, we see that God created man in His own image, both male and female. He blessed them and told them to reproduce, subdue the earth and take dominion over every living thing. It's clear that man and woman were created with specific purposes in mind. It's also important to keep in mind that God created us in His image. Just knowing we are created in the image of God is the beginning of being able to understand why we are here and what we are supposed to do. We will discuss in more detail shortly the differences in our roles and how that applies to our marriage.

Genesis 2:7
[7] then the LORD God formed the man of dust from the ground and breathed into his nostrils the breath of life, and the man became a living creature. (ESV)

Genesis 2:18-25
[18] Then the LORD God said, "It is not good that the man should be alone; I will make him a helper fit for him." [19] Now out of the ground the LORD God had formed every beast of the field and every bird of the heavens and brought them to the man to see what he would call them. And whatever the man called every living creature, that was its name. [20] The man gave names to all livestock and to the birds of the heavens and to every beast of the field. But for Adam there was not found a helper fit for him. [21] So the LORD God caused a deep sleep to fall upon the man, and while he slept took one of his ribs and closed up its place with flesh. [22] And the rib that the LORD God had taken from the man he made into a woman and brought her to the man. [23] Then the man said, "This at last is bone of my bones and flesh of my flesh; she shall be called Woman, because she was taken out of Man." [24] Therefore a man shall leave his father and his mother and hold fast to his wife, and they shall become one flesh. [25] And the man and his wife were both naked and were not ashamed. (ESV)

In Genesis 2:18-25 we see that God did not create man and woman at the same time or from the same ingredients. He created Adam out of the dust of the Earth. It wasn't until after Adam had seen and named every living creature that God pronounced it was not good for man to be alone.

This is a very significant point. God determined that man needed someone else comparable to him. We see that God created Eve to be a "help meet" (help mate) for him. Next we see that God created Eve not from the dust of the ground where she would be a separate creation, but from a rib bone of Adam. Eve was created out of Adam's side. She was not created from his head where she would be neither over him nor from his feet where she would be beneath him. She was created to come along side Adam as his partner. She was created to be there to help Adam fulfill the Will of God.

Adam was created first in the full image of God. But when God determined that Adam needed a companion, He put Adam to sleep and then He removed one of Adam's ribs and created a separate female being. He then presented this female being to Adam to name just as he named all the other creatures. Adam named her "Woman" because she was taken "out of Man". This is when God established the institution of marriage. We see in Genesis. 2:24-25 that God is referring to "the man and his wife". Another very significant point is that in verse 24 we see that a man is to leave his father and mother and cleave (be faithful) to his wife thus becoming one flesh.

Recognizing that Adam and Eve were originally "one flesh", we can see that God intended for them to remain one flesh. It's interesting to note that He also warned about potential problems with in-laws even though Adam and Eve only had Father God as their "parent". We will spend much more time with in-law issues in a later chapter. We should also note that God provided the wife that He wanted Adam to have. God needs to be involved in the search for a wife so that a man gets the right one.

GOD'S ORDER IN MARRIAGE

1 Corinthians 11:2-3
Head Coverings
[2] Now I commend you because you remember me in everything and maintain the traditions even as I delivered them to you. [3] But I want you to understand that the head of every man is Christ, the head of a wife is her husband, and the head of Christ is God. (ESV)

Within the institution of marriage, God established a certain vertical relationship. As we see in 1 Corinthians 11: 3, Christ is the head of every man; man is the head of the woman; and God the Father is the head of Christ. Any time this order is out of alignment, there will be all sorts of contention and strife. It's imperative that, in a Godly marriage, Christ be the head of every man. The man's role is to be the Prophet and Priest in his home. Let's look at Ephesians 5 below."

Ephesians 5:21-33
[21] submitting to one another out of reverence for Christ.
Wives and Husbands
[22] Wives, submit to your own husbands, as to the Lord. [23] For the husband is the head of the wife even as Christ is the head of the church, his body, and is himself

its Savior. [24] Now as the church submits to Christ, so also wives should submit in everything to their husbands.[25] Husbands, love your wives, as Christ loved the church and gave himself up for her, [26] that he might sanctify her, having cleansed her by the washing of water with the word, [27] so that he might present the church to himself in splendor, without spot or wrinkle or any such thing, that she might be holy and without blemish. [28] In the same way husbands should love their wives as their own bodies. He who loves his wife loves himself. [29] For no one ever hated his own flesh, but nourishes and cherishes it, just as Christ does the church, [30] because we are members of his body. [31] "Therefore a man shall leave his father and mother and hold fast to his wife, and the two shall become one flesh." [32] This mystery is profound, and I am saying that it refers to Christ and the church. [33] However, let each one of you love his wife as himself, and let the wife see that she respects her husband. (ESV)

It's very clear that husbands are to be the head of their wife **AS** Christ is the head of the church (which is His bride). As it states in verse 24, the church is subject to Christ, therefore let the wives be subject to their own husbands in everything. This scripture goes back to the book of Genesis Chapter 3 which relates both stories of Eve being deceived by the serpent and Adam taking a bite of the forbidden apple. We see below where God is putting a curse directly on Eve. Besides pain in childbirth, her desire will be for her husband but he will be her master. God does not put a curse on Adam, but he does curse the ground so that now Adam will have to toil to make a living from it.

Genesis 3:16-24

[16] To the woman he said, "I will surely multiply your pain in childbearing; in pain you shall bring forth children. Your desire shall be contrary to your husband, but he shall rule over you." [17] And to Adam he said, "Because you have listened to the voice of your wife and have eaten of the tree of which I commanded you, 'You shall not eat of it,' cursed is the ground because of you; in pain you shall eat of it all the days of your life; [18] thorns and thistles it shall bring forth for you; and you shall eat the plants of the field. [19] By the sweat of your face you shall eat bread, till you return to the ground, for out of it you were taken; for you are dust, and to dust you shall return." [20] The man called his wife's name Eve, because she was the mother of all living. [21] And the LORD God made for Adam and for his wife garments of skins and clothed them. [22] Then the LORD God said, "Behold, the man has become like one of us in knowing good and evil. Now, lest he reach out his hand and take also of the tree of life and eat, and live forever—" [23] therefore the LORD God sent him out from the garden of Eden to work the ground from which he was taken. [24] He drove out the man, and at

the east of the garden of Eden he placed the cherubim and a flaming sword that turned every way to guard the way to the tree of life. (ESV)

What we find in verse 21 is that God made clothing for Adam and Eve out of animal skins. When they had sinned and became aware that they were naked, they tried to use fig leaves to cover themselves. God sacrificed some animals so that Adam and Eve's sin could be covered. We see that God requires blood to be shed as a sacrifice for sin as a preview of Christ shedding His blood on the cross for the sins of mankind.

In a Godly marriage, we need to understand that each one of us is a sinner. No matter where we are in our walk with God. We put our full faith and trust in the Lord and not in our spouse. Our spouse is to be seen as a gift from God. Our spouse will let us down sooner or later and we are to remember that we are there as a partner. We are to be there to pick each other up when the other one falls. Our spouse is not our enemy, but our partner in a fight against a common enemy – the Devil.

Here's a diagram which represents the priority order of relationships found in a marriage.

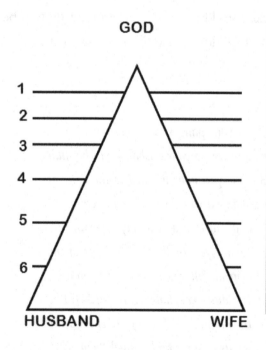

In picture form, a triangle is typically used to represent the priority of relationships as they should be in a Godly marriage. (The "Priority Pyramid")

1. Each spouse's ETERNAL relationship with God

2. The covenant FOR LIFE marriage relationship

3. The parental STEWARDSHIP PERIOD raising God's children (approximately 18-25 years)

4. The relationship with other family and friends FOR A SEASON

5. The relationship with your employer or business FOR A SEASON

6. The relationship with your ministry. Your first ministry should be your spouse and then your immediate family.

God is to be your most important relationship. It's eternal. This is also called the vertical relationship. Each spouse needs to constantly be working on this relationship. When this is in good order, the next relationship (the marriage or horizontal relationship) works best. The marriage is to be a blood covenant, not a contract nor a commitment. A blood covenant is one entered into with God and can only be terminated by death. Malachi 2:16 tells us that God hates divorce, so our goal should be to honor the covenant you have made before God and with your spouse.

Your children come next in the list of priorities. You do not own them. You are to be good stewards of God's children and to teach them for a period of time and then let them go to create their own families. When they are taught well, they will be able to function well on their own.

After your children comes the relationship with your extended family members and friends. You can't pick your relatives, so frequently God will use them to test your Christian walk. Friends are often only for a season. Some seasons are short while others are life long. You have to listen to the prompting of the Holy Spirit as to when a season is over. Understand that God has a purpose for each person that He brings into your life. That purpose may be for you to learn from them or you might be the one chosen to teach them.

Next on the priority list is the relationship with your employer. You're to have an abundant life, but you need to keep your job in perspective and not turn it into an idol.

The same goes with your ministry. Serving God is a great calling, but God still wants your home to be in order before you try to do any ministry work. Our spouse and our family are a higher priority ministry than any other ministry.

BE IMITATORS OF CHRIST

Finally, to get the most out of your marriage, be imitators of Christ. Get to know Him intimately. Spend time praying with your spouse on a daily basis. Prayer creates intimacy in three areas: the one to whom you pray, the one with whom you pray and the one(s) for whom you pray. When you exercise God's Grace and Mercy with your spouse, you can cover a multitude of sins that occur in your marriage. Like Christ – let him who is without sin cast the first stone.

Give up your right to be offended. Remember what Christ said as He was dying on the cross – "Father, forgive them, for they know not what they do." He was innocent, yet was able to forgive those who were killing Him because He knew they really didn't understand the big picture. How can you as a sinner stand and accuse your spouse as a sinner without being judged yourself?

MARRIAGE FUNDAMENTALS

- Man was created from dust with a need for a relationship.
- Woman was created from man to fill man's need for a relationship.
- Man is to cleave (be faithful) to that wife and become one flesh with her.
- Marriage is a blood covenant - not a contract or commitment.
- God has established an order of priorities for marriage and family.
- Pray together daily.
- Give up your right to be offended and be quick to extend forgiveness.

EXERCISES FOR LESSON 2

1. Describe how Adam and Eve were created differently. Why is that significant?

2. Why did Adam name his helpmate "Woman"?

3. God needs to be involved in the search for a wife so that a _____ gets the right _____.

4. What were the consequences of Adam's and Eve's sin? See Genesis 3:24.

CHAPTER 3

PREPARE A ROAD MAP FOR YOUR MARRIAGE JOURNEY

It's easy to always hit the target if you shoot first and then paint the bullseye around where the bullet went. Life is not that simple. Neither is marriage. It is necessary to have some idea of where you want to go in order to figure out how to get there. Preparing to enter into a blended family situation, as in any marriage, requires lots of prayer and planning beforehand to have a chance of succeeding. Playing marriage by ear and just seeing where you end up is a good way to end up in failure.

For a marriage to succeed, especially a marriage creating a blended family, you need to communicate with your future spouse and agree on where you want the marriage to go. The setting of goals and reaching agreement on them is critical. There is power in agreement. Goals that have been agreed upon give you the ability to work as one-flesh toward a common mission. Not having common goals leads to each individual working on their own personal mission. This allows the enemy an opportunity to create division in the marriage. You will eventually see your spouse as a hindrance to what you want to accomplish instead of working together to accomplish the same things.

Successful marriages require a covenant mentality. There needs to be a spirit of permanence. You have to know going in that no matter what, you and your spouse are going to go through whatever trials and tribulations God allows you to experience. His intention is that you will pick one another up as one falls. He expects you to make Him your tower of strength and your place of refuge when things are tough. The enemy of your soul wants you to cower in fear and to run away from God as a way to avoid the trials.

GOAL SETTING

What is a goal? A goal is simply something you determine in your mind today to make happen in reality in the future. Goals need to be specific, measurable, attainable, realistic and timely.

Being specific about your goal creates enough detail to be able to develop a plan of action. Setting a completion date is critical. You need to be able to measure your progress against the plan that you just developed to know if you are staying on schedule. Setting a goal that is impossible to attain ultimately results in failure, which then leads to never setting another goal. Realistic goals that are consistently met create a positive feeling of self-worth. That allows you to continually make progress towards the overall plan you created with your spouse for your journey through life together. Create short-term, medium-term and long-term goals.

Short-term goals are the goals that can keep you going while you're working on the, medium and long-term goals. They should be something you can accomplish in three to six months. Once the goal has been met, set another one. They keep you moving in the right direction and give you that sense of accomplishment that encourages your spirit to push through the tough times you might face on the longer-term goals. Short-term goals could include anything from a small purchase to a family weekend getaway.

Medium-term goals require a little more prayerful thought and planning to achieve. These goals generally could take a year or more of action to fulfill. You might need to stick to a budget to be able to pay off a particular credit card, save for a new set of tires for the car or even be able to get a newer car. It might take a year of planning to take the family on road trip of a week or two.

Long-term goals are generally the five to ten year (or longer) goals. These would include things such as home purchases, plans to start a new business, saving for retirement or career path changes. Long-term goals require much more prayer to make sure they are in-line with God's Will for you. He needs to be and wants to be a big part of your entire life, so He needs to be included in the process. Be willing to make adjustments to the plan as you hear God's calling on your life.

In a blended family situation, setting goals early is very important. Gathering the family together to set goals is a good way to start the blended family off on the right foot. Each member of the new blended family should have their own personal set of goals. This promotes a positive environment where everyone in the family has something they can strive for.

Knowing what your family members' goals are also gives you the ability to do positive things for them to help them achieve their goals. If you're helping them, they are more likely to help you. In addition to individual goals, there should be family goals and marriage goals. A great way to promote the setting of goals is to find pictures that represent what the goals are and put then in a prominent place so all the family members can be reminded of them on a daily basis. The refrigerator is a great place to post goals. You probably have several magnets stuck to the 'fridge anyway. You might as well put them to good use.

The down-side to setting goals is that, in a blended family, you will possibly have a very rebellious child to deal with – one who refuses to be part of the process. It's possible they will be anti-everything that you and your new spouse are trying to accomplish. This is where it is vital for the husband and wife to stick to God's Priority Pyramid and be in agreement as to how to deal with this potentially volatile situation. Work out a "Plan A" in advance so that you don't have to fallback to "Plan B" after you're married. Hopefully, you will be blessed with step-children that appreciate you being in their life.

One of the most difficult situation to handle in a blended family is how to handle discipline of the other spouse's child. It's absolutely necessary to be in agreement about who is going to do what. It should be agreed upon before the wedding that the children will be "our" children rather than "mine" or "yours". When child ownership plays into the equation, the house is immediately divided and conflict will arise. *Mark 3:24–25 [24] If a kingdom is divided against itself, that kingdom cannot stand. [25] And if a house is divided against itself, that house will not be able to stand. (ESV).* Other than finances, the disagreement over child discipline is probably the second most common reason for divorce in remarriages.

EX-SPOUSES AND/OR EX-GRANDPARENTS

Another part of your road map for your marriage needs to include reaching agreement on how to deal with ex-spouses and ex-grandparents. This is an area that really needs a lot of open and honest communication with a large dose of prayerful consideration prior to the wedding. This is where "for better or worse" usually becomes "or worse". When children are involved, you need to lay out boundaries around the necessary relationship with an ex-spouse or ex-grandparents.

First and foremost, as a Christian, you should be making every effort to create a peaceful relationship with your ex. Unfortunately, due to the circumstances surrounding the divorce and whether or not the ex is a Christian, the ex may not be willing to make peace but would rather make war. An ex-spouse that is out for revenge puts incredible stress on any remarriage. It will take much prayer as a couple to survive the trials and tribulations brought about by an ex-spouse that wants more than anything to see your new marriage fail. This scripture should be memorized by those entering into a blended family - *Matthew 5:43–44 Love Your Enemies*

[43] "You have heard that it was said, 'You shall love your neighbor and hate your enemy.' [44] But I say to you, Love your enemies and pray for those who persecute you, (ESV)

Never speak badly about your ex especially to your children. Ephesians 4:25-32 shows us that we have no business speaking or even thinking badly about another person.

> *[25] Therefore, having put away falsehood, let each one of you speak the truth with his neighbor, for we are members one of another. [26] Be angry and do not sin; do not let the sun go down on your anger, [27] and give no opportunity to the devil. [28] Let the thief no longer steal, but rather let him labor, doing honest work with his own hands, so that he may have something to share with anyone in need. [29] Let no corrupting talk come out of your mouths, but only such as is good for building up, as fits the occasion, that it may give grace to those who hear. [30] And do not grieve the Holy Spirit of God, by whom you were sealed for the day of redemption. [31] Let all bitterness and wrath and anger and clamor and slander be put away from you, along with all malice. [32] Be kind to one another, tenderhearted, forgiving one another, as God in Christ forgave you. (ESV)*

Ex-grandparents, like the ex-spouse are still the blood relatives and have certain legal rights and expectations for visitation. Unless there is a possibility of a child being harmed while in their custody, allowances need to be made and grace extended by the new step-parent to accommodate visitation. Adherence to any court rulings regarding child custody, support and visitation is a must.

REBELLIOUS TEENS OR IMMATURE ADULT CHILDREN

An area of great strain on a new blended family relationship involves the outright rebellion against the new marriage by the children from either parent. This deliberate negative behavior is often a test to see how strong the marital relationship really is. That is why the Priority Pyramid needs to be put into effect and adhered to with all the strength you can muster. This type of behavior is one of the most common causes for

remarriages to fail. The new spouses have not worked out an agreement for a plan of action to handle such behavior so the child gets the upper hand and quickly drives a wedge between the parents.

The Priority Pyramid sets the standard by which any family needs to strive for. It puts all the relationships in the proper order to achieve and maintain a Godly household. When the marriage can withstand the test of fire through the blatant rebellion from one or more children in a blended family, the husband and wife become stronger in their relationship. When the children see how secure that relationship is, they generally respond favorably to the new marriage. If they don't eventually come around, it's their problem, not yours. Remember, everyone is responsible for their own actions.

Once again, it's important to realize that bringing yours, mine and ours into a smoothly running operation takes a lot of work, courage, patience, commitment and prayer. You're the salmon swimming upstream and there are lots of bears along the way just waiting to devour you. Survival depends on God's help and a large dose of His Grace.

Another sticky situation is when one or both spouses have adult children that just can't seem to get their life together and live a responsible life on their own. The target group here is the 25- to 40-year olds. In many cases, the parents did not spend the time to really teach them proper life skills. There are a couple of generations of children now whose parents were too busy to give them good parenting so instead, they gave them everything else money could buy. When they call and have no job, no money or their own marriage is falling apart, the parental instinct kicks in and your first thought is to bail them out of their predicament. This puts strain on the new marital relationship due to frequently having to "save" the adult child from the consequences of their lifestyle choices. Obviously, true emergencies require parental intervention, but often it's just easier to throw money at a problem in hopes that it will disappear. Many times, the adult child takes advantage of the parent and knows exactly how to manipulate them. Resentment is often the result seen in the step-parent when the birth parent is too quickly persuaded to hand over cash to fix a problem.

You've probably heard the phrase "tough love". Sometimes, the right thing to do is to let the child fall on their face and suffer the consequences of their own choices. That is how God corrects bad behavior in His kids. He hates pride. Sometimes, He lets them get to the end of their rope, so that they have no other choice but to repent and turn to Him. In God's economy, you reap what you sow. If you sow bad choices, you will reap the consequences. There's no escaping God's principles. In a blended family, it's usually easier for the step-parent to see the need for tough love than it is the birth parent. This creates a point of contention because now there is disagreement. You need to go back once again to the Priority Pyramid to understand why it is so important to keep all the family relationships in the proper order or else there will be disagreement and division that the enemy can use to destroy you.

AGREE ON A PLAN FOR DISCIPLINE OF "OUR" CHILDREN

It's wise to work out a plan for discipline of the children that you can both agree on before the wedding. Make sure you both see all the children as "ours". Keep the marriage elevated above the parent/child relationship. Once the plan has been agreed to, stick to it. You would be wise to write down all the things you agree to. Also, go over the agreed upon plan with the children before the wedding. It will save you many headaches down the road. As has been stated before, there is power in agreement. When there is disagreement, especially after the wedding, it is much more difficult to reach a place of agreement. Kids, as much as they hate to admit it, prefer to know where their boundaries are. They don't always behave like they appreciate boundaries, but it shows them that you care enough about them to set limits for them to abide by.

Make sure the plan sets limits that are age appropriate. If you have teens, make sure they have a curfew and that they check in from time to time. They need to be taught that with freedom comes responsibility. If you can't be responsible, you start losing your freedom. They also need to understand that there are consequences for their actions. Don't let them see themselves as victims when they simply made bad choices. Teach them about personal accountability. The best way is to teach them is to show them through your own actions. There will be many opportunities to extend grace to your kids when they start being more independent. You should love them through their mistakes as much as possible rather than tearing them down when you talk to them. Be strong and wise. Get very familiar with the book of Proverbs. It will give you many gems to use with your children.

HAVE A COVENANT MENTALITY

The best chance for any marriage to survive, especially a marriage creating a blended family, is for both you and your future spouse to enter into the marriage with a covenant mentality. Be serious about your vows to each other. Know going in that there will be many challenges to your marriage. Life is full of interesting twists and turns. All things are possible through Christ who strengthens you. All those trials and tribulations that you may encounter are temporary rough spots that God allows you to work through with the intention of getting to know and trust Him better and to become more spiritually mature.

Marriage can be very rewarding for both spouses if they understand and value the concept of covenant. This understanding, and being in agreement regarding this understanding, allows each person to have the freedom to be what God created them to be. You are free from the condemnation of the law and can now live in the freedom of God's Grace. You can choose to extend to your new spouse the Grace that you receive from God. Divorce is removed from the dictionary and is never spoken no matter how intense the trials may be. A successful marriage requires frequent renewing of your mind. You can never allow yourself to see your spouse as your enemy. Your spouse should be considered a very precious gift from God of which you need to be a good steward. Don't forget to keep in mind that marriage is spiritual warfare. The Devil is always trying to divide you. It's one way for him to try to hurt God.

EXERCISES FOR LESSON 3

1. Why is it important to set goals?

2. What are the three types of goals you should set?

3. Describe how you would handle visitation rights for an ex-grandparent.

4. Describe how you would handle an ex-spouse that is deliberately causing you and your new spouse problems.

CHAPTER 4

"WHO'S THE BOSS?" - FROM SINGLE PARENT TO "MARRIED WITH CHILDREN"

Are you old enough to remember the two sit-coms that are referenced in the title of this chapter? In the show "Who's the Boss?" a man worked as a housekeeper for a female "boss". That's not so unusual these days, but in the mid-'80's to early '90's it was more of the exception. In the show "Married with Children" (1987-1997) you start seeing (on TV) the destruction of the role of the husband and the father. If you're even older, you may remember the "ideal" families on TV – "Leave it to Beaver" (1957-1963) and Father Knows Best" (1954-1960) . This lesson will explain God's plan for a husband/father and a wife/mother. Issues pertaining to a blended family will be pointed out in more detail.

One of the reasons that there are so many blended families being created today is that sons no longer have Godly fathers to teach them how to be Godly men. There have been several generations now where the males have been taught to "get in touch with their feminine side". There has been a progressively downhill slide in the portrayal of a husband and father figure in TV and movies. He is often portrayed as lazy, inept, not very smart or incapable of making a decision. A husband/father in the media rarely is given any respect.

This lesson will describe the roles of the husband/father and wife/mother in the context of a Christian family. If you've been on your own for any length of time raising "your" kids, you've grown accustomed to doing things your way. You've also grown accustomed to performing both mother and father roles. The big question then becomes: How do you allow someone else to have any level of control over your life or your children? This is where many blended families run into trouble. Each spouse wants to maintain control over their own kids. On the surface, it would appear to make sense. However, this approach is contrary to God's order as described in the Priority Pyramid.

In a blended family, you have to stick to the proper order of relationship priorities. A husband needs to know that after God, he is the most important one in his wife's life. Likewise, a wife needs to know that after God, she is the most important to her husband. For any marriage to really work well, it needs to be God-centered. When it becomes child-centered, the opportunities for resentment to arise in the spouses increase exponentially. When it's all about the children, the marriage suffers because it gets neglected. When the marriage is not getting the attention is needs, it starts to die. This is why so many marriages end up in trouble when the nest is empty. The marital relationship has been focused on the kids for so long that the husband and wife barely know each other any more.

So, how do you move from being the boss to being married with children? Now that you understand the priorities of family relationships, you should know enough to set goals that will allow you to get your relationships in the proper order in a certain amount of time. God expects you to grow and keep growing in spiritual maturity. Marriage, especially in a blended situation, provides an endless supply of opportunities to mature. Being Christ-like, having an attitude of dependence on God, being humble and gentle, will serve you well in creating a successful blended family.

Reaching agreement on who is going to be responsible for what in the new household should be done before the wedding. It's not about certain things being a man's job or a woman's job, but you should determine which of you has the greatest gift in certain areas. Finance is a good example. Some people really like to work with numbers and some hate it with a passion. Let the person that is good at it and enjoys it, do it.

The following puts into perspective the role of a husband/father and a wife/mother. It applies to any marriage, but it is very important to keep this in perspective when blending a new family from two existing families. Two families, both used to being led by a single parent, are now trying to blend into one family with two parents. Who's going to lead now? See how the "mantle of leadership" should be worn in a two-parent family according to the plan God set forth in Scripture.

2 Kings 2:13
[13] And he took up the cloak of Elijah that had fallen from him and went back and stood on the bank of the Jordan. (ESV)

This verse refers to Elisha picking up the mantle that Elijah threw down as he (Elijah) was being carried off into Heaven in a chariot of fire.

A mantle was the official garment worn by a prophet. The mantle immediately marked a man as a prophet and spokesman of God. It let people know that there had been sacrifice and a commitment to God. A prophet's life was not a life of luxury. The mantle he wore represented a man's gift, his calling by God, and the purpose for which God had called him.

Going back to the creation of the institution of marriage, you saw where God cursed the ground and told Adam he would have to work the land to survive and provide for himself and his wife. God cursed Eve so that (in addition to pain in childbirth) she would want to be equal in leadership to her husband but was told by God that she would have to live in submission to her husband. She was created from Adam to be a helpmate not his supervisor. Having been created from a rib, it was intended for her to be one who would come along side and be a helper and encourager.

Ever since Adam, men have had a natural tendency towards laziness. If given the chance, many men would gladly give up wearing the mantle and the responsibility that goes with it. Women have a natural tendency to want to be in charge. That sounds like a perfect solution to the problem, right? Women want to be in charge and men are usually eager to give up the steering wheel. So, what naturally happens in a marriage is the husband chooses to not wear his mantle and leaves it lying on the floor.

The natural wife feels insecure. She feels a need to pick up the mantle and put it on to regain some sense of security. Someone has to be in charge, right? However, when this situation arises, what naturally happens is that the husband resents his wife when she inevitably tries to become his parole officer. Likewise, the wife resents her husband for putting the responsibility of the family on her shoulders. Eventually, the resentment builds to a level that creates such hostility that divorce seems to be the only answer. The husband needs to accept his roles as prophet, priest and king and the responsibility that goes with them. His purposes are to guide, guard and govern.

Try to visualize this example of wearing the mantle –

A couple is in their best Sunday outfits. The husband has on a very nice, custom-tailored suit and the wife is wearing one of her best designer dresses. All of a sudden, the husband, in his natural state of being, decides his mantle is getting too heavy for him. He takes it off and just drops it on the floor. The wife, in her natural state of being bends down and picks it up and puts it on over her designer dress.

The husband feels more comfortable now that he does not have so much weight on his shoulders. But now, the wife is feeling the extra weight of the mantle that she has picked up. It doesn't look good and doesn't come close to fitting her since it was tailor made for her husband. The shoulders are too wide and the sleeves are too long. It ruins the sleek lines of her designer dress. A wife is to be the glory of her husband but her husband is to be the image and glory of God.

1 Corinthians 11:7

[7] For a man ought not to cover his head, since he is the image and glory of God, but woman is the glory of man. (ESV)

Most of you have probably heard the phrase "Behind every great man there is a great woman." A man derives the majority of his self-worth through what he does. Therefore, he needs his wife to be for him and not against him. The average man will only accomplish things in life according to the level of belief his wife has in him. He will invariably live up to her expectations of him. If they are high and she is edifying him, he will strive to meet those expectations. If her expectations are low and she is tearing him down, he will accomplish very little.

A good Scriptural reference for this is Proverbs 14:1.

Proverbs 14:1

[1] The wisest of women builds her house, but folly with her own hands tears it down. (ESV)

If a wife has high expectations but a low level of faith in her husband being able to meet them, both spouses will be disappointed and resentful. If the wife has spent sufficient time getting to know her husband, she will be able to know how to encourage and bless him and he will be able to accomplish much more in life than he would ever have been able to on his own.

As we read Proverbs 12:4 we see a woman can be either of two very different things to her husband. One attribute is highly desirable while the other is like a cancer.

Proverbs 12:4

[4] An excellent wife is the crown of her husband, but she who brings shame is like rottenness in his bones. (ESV)

Blending a family, especially after a divorce situation, requires that both the husband and wife be aware of the impact they can have on each other and any children that might be involved. They need to understand the power of their words and their actions towards one another. In many gift shops there is often a sign that says, "If Momma ain't happy, ain't nobody happy." That sounds very similar to Proverbs 21:19.

Proverbs 21:19
[19] It is better to live in a desert land than with a quarrelsome and fretful woman. (ESV)

The husband, as mentioned earlier is to be the prophet, priest and king. His role as prophet is to speak the Word of God and teach his family what the Word of God says about them and the way they should behave.

His role as priest is to provide the spiritual leadership and covering for his wife and his family. When he is fulfilling his role as priest, it creates an atmosphere of security and comfort for his wife. When she's at ease, the temperature in the home is usually at a comfortable level. When that's not being done, the Enemy has easier access to alter the thermostat and can make the temperature either too hot to handle or frigidly cold.

Men will do almost anything to please a woman when she is encouraging and has positive things to say about him. Wives need to beware that if they are generally tearing down and saying negative things, their husband will be easily tempted by a flattering female. Men especially need to be putting on the full armor of God (see Ephesians 6) to avoid these temptations. Proverbs 5:3-9 has a lot to say regarding this issue –

Proverbs 5:3–9
[3] For the lips of a forbidden woman drip honey, and her speech is smoother than oil, [4] but in the end she is bitter as wormwood, sharp as a two-edged sword. [5] Her feet go down to death; her steps follow the path to Sheol; [6] she does not ponder the path of life; her ways wander, and she does not know it. [7] And now, O sons, listen to me, and do not depart from the words of my mouth. [8] Keep your way far from her, and do not go near the door of her house, [9] lest you give your honor to others and your years to the merciless, (ESV)

A successful blended family needs to move beyond those natural tendencies of the flesh and move into the supernatural. You need a third party to help you perform in that supernatural realm in order to fulfill your God-intended roles and responsibilities. That third party is Jesus Christ, who came to help you live an abundant life. When the husband's relationship with Christ is in good standing, he will speak life and blessings over his wife and family. When the wife's relationship is in good standing, she will understand her role as the multifaceted helper who is there to edify and strengthen her husband and nurture her children. They will both understand that they are there to pick each other up should one fall - not kick them while they are down.

Ecclesiastes 4:12

[12] And though a man might prevail against one who is alone, two will withstand him—a threefold cord is not quickly broken. (ESV)

This Scripture gives you a good idea of how important it is for Christ to be in the middle of a marriage. It makes the relationship so much stronger when Christ is at the head of both the husband and the wife. As was mentioned in Lesson 2, it's vital that the husband and wife relationship be elevated above the parent/child relationship. When both spouses are spending time in God's Word, praying together daily and listening to what God has to say< there will be a high level of intimacy, peace and unity in the relationship. It takes time and effort from each spouse to make a marriage work. Marriage is not a 50%-50% arrangement. It has to be a relationship in which each party gives 100% effort to make it succeed.

When each spouse is living up to their God-given roles and responsibilities, the children see that there is peace and security in the home. They learn about the relationship you are all to have with Christ. They can see that the relationship that Father and Mother have with each other resembles that which Christ has with His bride (the Church) and it sets a great example for them to take into their own life down the road. They will be better prepared to understand God's grace and forgiveness because they will have received both from their earthly father and mother.

One example of how the roles and responsibilities work best in a Christ-centered family can be taken from the world of big business. When we look at a corporation, there is always the Chairman of the Board, the Board members, the Chief Executive Officer (CEO) and the Chief Operations Officer (COO). When we apply this structure to a family we have God being the Chairman of the Board. He is fully responsible for the overall success of the company. He is the ultimate authority in the company and the buck stops with him. He establishes the overriding vision and mission for the company.

The Chairman of the Board gives the husband (CEO) the direction he wants the company to go. The CEO's job is to take the vision from the Chairman and share it with the rest of the company (the family) and get their buy-in. The CEO then communicates daily with the wife (COO) to determine the various tasks that need to be completed to get the job done. It's the COO's responsibility to ensure that the day-to-day tasks get done so that the vision can become a reality. Families that put in the effort to build each other up and accept their roles and responsibilities can create a well-oiled machine that produces great fruit for the Kingdom of God.

EXERCISES FOR LESSON 4

1. Is it always the husband's role to control the family's finances? Explain.

2. Explain how a strong marriage is like a 3-stranded cord. What does the 3rd strand represent?

3. Fill in the blanks. 'A wise woman builds her _____. A foolish woman _____ hers down with her own _____".

4. Describe how a corporation and a family are similar. Explain the duties of each of the primary 'Executives'.

CHAPTER 5

HOW TO BE A GOOD STEP-PARENT

With the right attitude, there are many blessings to be gained by being a good step-parent. If you have a bad attitude, being a step-parent can quickly turn into a nightmare. Becoming a parent is not always a choice, but the Bible is clear that children are a gift and a blessing from God. Children should be treated accordingly. Becoming a step-parent gives you the opportunity to choose the children you want to help raise. With the proper edification by the birth parent, the children should see you (the step-parent) as a person that chose to be part of their life - not someone who invaded and came to occupy their territory.

You, as the step-parent, can not allow yourself to be jealous of the relationship that the children have with their birth parent. This applies to both spouses that are becoming a blended family. There can only be one set of rules. All children in the family have to be "our" children. You can not treat your own kids any better than your new spouse's children. That is a sure way to create division in the home. As you have seen with the Pyramid, if either spouse regards their relationship with any of the children at a higher level than the marriage, there will be problems.

One way to speed up the process of being accepted by your new spouse's children is to be a servant. That does not mean you have to give them whatever they ask for just to get on their good side. As a servant, you not only serve your new spouse as you serve the Lord, but you do what you can to be a positive influence for the children. Demonstrate Christ-likeness to your new family. Show your spouse and the children that you have integrity and that you do what you say you are going to do. This earns you respect. As the new person in this relationship, you can't immediately assert your "adult" authority. You have to take the time to build a trusting relationship with your new spouse and the children. When they trust and respect you, they will be more likely to submit to your leadership. No one cares how much you know until they know how much you care. Get to know the children. If the children are young, get down on your knees so you can look into their eyes and also to see things from their perspective.

AGE AND GENDER AFFECT HOW THE CHILDREN BLEND

Children under 10 –

Children under 10 years old often adjust more easily because they thrive best when the family unit is strong and cohesive. They tend to be more willing to accept a new adult in the household. They generally will be more competitive for their own parent's attention. Since they are younger, they will require more attention on a daily basis.

Adolescents aged 10-15 –

You will face more challenges because this is the age group seems to have the most difficulty adjusting to a new parent in the family. You will need to spend more time bonding with this age group especially before you attempt to become a disciplinarian. Often, kids in this age group do not demonstrate feelings openly but could be even more sensitive than the younger children in needing love, support, attention or discipline.

Teenagers 15 and up –

Teenagers at this age are starting to form their own personal identity and will often start pulling away from the family unit. You will have much less opportunity to influence them as a step-parent. Most of your time will be spent in the earning mutual respect mode. You may be blessed to have a teen that enjoys family life and is not always looking for ways to make your life miserable. They generally still want to feel needed and important but will rarely let you know about. It interferes with their desire to be independent.

In a blended family, the biggest difference from a first marriage is that you don't have any time to just be a couple when you are first starting out. From Day One you are parents and now you have to figure out how to be a parent to someone else's child. If you haven't done your homework, you will probably fail the test. Even if you fail the first time or two, keep taking the test. Stay close to God and eventually you'll be able to pass the test.

Take a look at a couple of good examples of Biblical step-parents. First, open the book of Matthew to Chapter 1 and read about one of the most significant step-dads in the Bible.

Matthew 1:18–25

The Birth of Jesus Christ

[18] Now the birth of Jesus Christ took place in this way. When his mother Mary had been betrothed to Joseph, before they came together she was found to be with child from the Holy Spirit. [19] And her husband Joseph, being a just man and unwilling to put her to shame, resolved to divorce her quietly. [20] But as he considered these things, behold, an angel of the Lord appeared to him in a dream, saying, "Joseph, son of David, do not fear to take Mary as your wife, for that which is conceived in her is from the Holy Spirit. [21] She will bear a son, and you shall call his name Jesus, for he will save his people from their sins." [22] All this took place to fulfill what the Lord had spoken by the prophet: [23] "Behold, the virgin shall conceive and bear a son, and they shall call his name Immanuel" (which means, God with us). [24] When Joseph woke from sleep, he did as the angel of the Lord commanded him: he took his wife, [25] but knew her not until she had given birth to a son. And he called his name Jesus. (ESV)

Another significant step-parent was Mordecai. He stepped up to raise Esther. Esther eventually became the Queen of the Persian Empire and risked her life to save the Jewish people from a plot to wipe them from the face of the Earth.

Esther 2:7

[7] He was bringing up Hadassah, that is Esther, the daughter of his uncle, for she had neither father nor mother. The young woman had a beautiful figure and was lovely to look at, and when her father and her mother died, Mordecai took her as his own daughter. (ESV)

At this point, make a distinction between being a mother or father and a mom or dad. For purposes of this lesson, a mother or father is simply the biological parent. A mom or dad is the person who chooses to love and raise their children, with the understanding that they are to be a good steward of God's children. A mom and dad realize that children are a gift from God and that they belong to Him. As parents you are to watch over them and raise them to be Godly offspring so that they can someday leave the nest and duplicate the process of raising a Godly family.

There are blessings from having children and there are blessings from raising Godly children.

Psalm 127:3

[3] Behold, children are a heritage from the LORD, the fruit of the womb a reward. (ESV)

Proverbs 23:24

[24] The father of the righteous will greatly rejoice; he who fathers a wise son will be glad in him. (ESV)

Proverbs 20:11

[11] Even a child makes himself known by his acts, by whether his conduct is pure and upright. (ESV)

Proverbs 17:6

[6] Grandchildren are the crown of the aged, and the glory of children is their fathers. (ESV)

Proverbs 29:21

[21] Whoever pampers his servant from childhood will in the end find him his heir. (ESV)

TEACHING, CORRECTION, DISCIPLINE AND PUNISHMENT

This section focuses on the teaching, correction, discipline and the necessity of punishment of children. Proverbs has many verses that speak to a parent on how to bring up their children.

An example of teaching can involve using some event that occurs in life, good or bad, and taking the time to explain to a child how that event could have happened. Naturally, this should be done in the context of a Christian world view as this is an opportunity to teach a child about who God is and how He works.

Besides behavioral things that will keep them safe and able to function in society, teach your children how to set goals, delayed gratification (seek God's Will) and how to handle money (good stewardship). Teach them about giving, sowing and reaping.

Correction is pointing out an error in behavior when a child has already been taught the right way to behave. If the error was a mistake, it's an opportunity to show grace and mercy. Teach them to confess and ask for forgiveness. Be quick to forgive them and praise them when they react quickly to the correction.

Discipline is doing the "right thing" repetitively over a period of time to reinforce the correct behavior which is desired. Boot camp in the military is an example of discipline. In a parenting situation, discipline (or chastisement) is sometimes needed when attempts to correct a behavior are deliberately ignored. Discipline requires consequences of appropriate severity so that the original teaching is reinforced. Discipline, by its nature, requires effort. Parents have to take time and be consistent with the agreed upon consequences to "disciple" their children. Certain conditions have to be met for a specified period of time until the desired behavior becomes "natural".

Punishment is something that should be reserved for the immediate termination of a negative behavior such as when a child is throwing a tantrum. Punishment normally does not result in long-term changes in a child's behavior. Punishment over an extended period can result in even more undesirable behaviors. It's a quick and easy way to deal with a problem in the short-term, as opposed to discipline that requires time and effort over an extended period of time. Tantrums often occur in public (but not always), so one of the first things you need to do is get the attention of the child so that you can take authority over them and show them you are in charge. An example of quick, deliberate action on your part creating just enough pain for the child that they stop the tantrum is to pinch them on the arm or leg. Pinching won't harm the child but let's them know their behavior is unsatisfactory. This works really well if you happen to be dining out in a nice restaurant because you can do the pinching under the table. Most children have figured out by the time they reach the age of three whether you are in charge or they are.

Through the following Proverbs, you can see that God intended for children to be treated the same way He treats His children. He blesses them when they are obedient and He corrects them with mercy when they disobey. You need to be diligent in speaking the Word of God to your children. You can see that you don't have to teach children to be foolish. It is something they are born with, but it can be beaten out of them. Spanking is part of God's plan for discipline according to Proverbs 22:15. Many parents today see spanking as being the same thing as child abuse. If you never have occasion to spank your child – Praise God! Most children are going to test your character as a parent. They will test you to see how serious you are about the boundaries you have established for them. A good spanking when the boundaries are pushed too far, reinforces the fact that there are consequences for bad choices. Finally, you see four Proverbs that say almost the same thing, so it must be extremely important to God. You see that you must pay attention, hear the Word of God, and not forget the wisdom that you have been given. God desires obedience much more than He wants sacrifice.

Proverbs 22:6

[6] Train up a child in the way he should go; even when he is old he will not depart from it. (ESV)

Proverbs 22:15

[15] Folly is bound up in the heart of a child, but the rod of discipline drives it far from him. (ESV)

Proverbs 23:13

[13] Do not withhold discipline from a child; if you strike him with a rod, he will not die. (ESV)

Proverbs 4:1

A Father's Wise Instruction

[1] Hear, O sons, a father's instruction, and be attentive, that you may gain insight, (ESV)

Proverbs 7:24

[24] And now, O sons, listen to me, and be attentive to the words of my mouth. (ESV)

Proverbs 8:32

[32] "And now, O sons, listen to me: blessed are those who keep my ways. (ESV)

You should be teaching your children manners. "Please" and "Thank You" should be frequent and automatic, but today it's almost a lost art. Teaching works best by showing your children how to do something, not just telling them. They learn more from catching than just hearing. Lead by example. As Christian parents, you *should* be imitators of Christ. Your children *will* be imitators of you.

EXERCISES FOR LESSON 5

1. Name the Biblical step-parents used as examples in this chapter. Can you name any others?

2. Fill in the blanks – "No one _____ how much you _____ until they _____ how much you _____.

3. Discuss why children are a blessing from God.

4. Write a short description of what your soon-to-be step-children might write about you if they had to write something for a school project. Would it be positive or negative?

CHAPTER 6

HANDLING FINANCES – USING THE 10-10-80 PRINCIPLE

The Bible has more references about money and what to do with it than any other topic. Even references to love come second to references to money. What people do with their money shows the condition of their heart and who their Lord is. Look at these Scriptures from 1st Timothy, Matthew and Deuteronomy.

1 Timothy 6:6–12

*[6] But godliness with contentment is great gain, [7] for we brought nothing into the world, and we cannot take anything out of the world. [8] But if we have food and clothing, with these we will be content. [9] But those who desire to be rich fall into temptation, into a snare, into many senseless and harmful desires that plunge people into ruin and destruction. **[10] For the love of money is a root of all kinds of evils. It is through this craving that some have wandered away from the faith and pierced themselves with many pangs.** [11] But as for you, O man of God, flee these things. Pursue righteousness, godliness, faith, love, steadfastness, gentleness. [12] Fight the good fight of the faith. Take hold of the eternal life to which you were called and about which you made the good confession in the presence of many witnesses. (ESV)*

Matthew 6:19–24

*[19] "Do not lay up for yourselves treasures on earth, where moth and rust destroy and where thieves break in and steal, [20] but lay up for yourselves treasures in heaven, where neither moth nor rust destroys and where thieves do not break in and steal. **[21] For where your treasure is, there your heart will be also**. [22] "The eye is the lamp of the body. So, if your eye is healthy, your whole body will be full of light, [23] but if your eye is bad, your whole body will be full of darkness. If then the light in you is darkness, how great is the darkness! **[24] "No one can serve two masters, for either he will hate the one and love the other, or he will be devoted to the one and despise the other. You cannot serve God and money**. (ESV)*

Deuteronomy 8:18

[18] You shall remember the LORD your God, for it is he who gives you power to get wealth, *that he may confirm his covenant that he swore to your fathers, as it is this day. (ESV)*

From these Scriptures you see that:

- God gives you the power to get wealth,
- The "love" of money is the root of all kinds of evil.
- What you do with your money proves the condition of your heart.

Money in and of itself is not good or evil. It's what you do with it and how you think about it that matters. When kept in the proper perspective, money can be a huge blessing to many and can be used to expand the Kingdom of God. If you first understand that everything you have belongs to God and is a gift from Him, you will have a good foundation to be able to handle your finances well. You don't own anything. You are expected to be a good steward of what God has given you to manage for Him.

A good rule of thumb is the 10-10-80 principle. Out of the 100% that God gives you, He expects you to give Him a tithe of 10%. That's 10% of the gross – not what you have left after taxes. This goes to the church (God's house) to care for widows and orphans and to expand the Kingdom. The next "10" is the 10% that you should pay yourself as way of building a savings or investment account. The "80" is the 80% that is left after you have paid God back and paid yourself. This is what you have left to live on.

Prior to getting married, you should create a budget. A budget is simply figuring out how much money you have to work with and what your expenses are. If there is money left over at the end of the month after all the expenses are paid, Congratulations! You are in a very select few that are actually living within your means. Unfortunately, the majority will have more month left at the end of the money and there will still be bills to pay. If this is you, you have two options. Increase your income to match your expenses or reduce your expenses to match your income. In many cases it requires some of both.

The first step to sound financial responsibility is creating your budget. You have to figure out where you are starting from to figure out what you have to do to get where you want to go. There are many examples of monthly budgets available on the internet. If you have a computer with a spreadsheet program, it makes it very simple to put your income in one column and you expenses in the other. Subtract the expenses from the income and determine what you have left over. Pray that the number does not have a minus sign in front of it.

Creating a budget to live by involves listing out everything that you spend money on. If you can, go back over the last few months and see where all your money has been spent. Budgets are not hard and fast, but often require making adjustments. You might be over-spending in certain areas and need to cut back to be able to cover expenses in another area. You should take a good look at your budget at least every quarter to make sure you are staying on track according to those goals you should have already set by now. The following "guidelines" represent some good ballpark ranges that you can use for the various categories of expenditures.

- Charitable Giving 10-15%
- Invest/Savings 5-10%
- Housing 25-35%
- Utilities 5-10%
- Food 5-15%
- Transportation 10-15%
- Medical 5-10%
- Clothing 2-7%
- Debt Payments 5-10%
- Misc. (Personal, Recreation, Life Ins.) 5-10%

You can't deal with finances without getting serious about credit card debt. If you are now or have ever been using a credit card just to make ends meet, you know it is only a matter of time before the credit runs out and you find yourself at a dead end with no where to go. With the extremely high interest rates on most cards, it is very difficult to ever get them paid off. The best philosophy is to put yourself on a cash and carry budget. Stop using the credit cards except in emergency situations. Stopping to get an iced mocha at the drive-thru is not an emergency. Credit card companies want to keep you in debt. Without your payments against your card balance, they have no income. By avoiding revolving debt, you can use that money that would be sent to the credit card company for other money-saving or money-making opportunities. Having high levels of credit card debt is similar to being in prison. As was mentioned earlier in 1st Timothy, the love of money is the root of all sorts of evil. When you allow the enemy to tempt you into spending money you don't have to impress people you don't like, you have allowed yourself to be put into bondage. Carrying a high level of debt also prevents you from using your money to benefit the Kingdom of God.

One of the reasons God hates divorce is that it destroys the family. Divorce robs God's children of much of their inheritance that they could have had if the divorce had not occurred. The only ones that benefit from divorce are the divorce lawyers. Divorce requires the division of assets and more often than not, leaves moms to raise the children with much less financial resources than what was available when the marriage was still intact. Many single-parent families struggle from day-to-day just to be able to eat or have a place to sleep. Children without fathers have a much higher rate of being put in jail than children that have (or had) a good relationship with their father.

Creating a blended family often brings together two people that have recently been through financial hardships. This frequently has caused at least one if not both parties to have major credit problems. In addition to bad credit, there is often a mountain of debt that is being carried by one or the other. This severely inhibits the ability to rebuild your assets (like buying a home). Financial stresses and disagreement over child discipline are the two most frequent reasons for remarriages to fail. Financial stress brings out and magnifies all the other issues that would normally stay hidden. Without monetary resources, you can no longer escape those issues and the "little foxes" eventually become the elephant in the room that can no longer be ignored.

The ideal situation is that of the one-flesh relationship. Finances work best when there is one account to which both spouses have access. There has to be frequent communication regarding the family's finances. There has to be agreement as to how the money is going to be spent. There needs to be a financial plan for the short and long-term. The Godly husband should be ultimately responsible for the overall financial health of the marriage and family. If he is gifted with being able to balance a checking account, then by all means he should do it. If the wife has the gift, she should take care of it. The key is the regular and open communication between the spouses as to the financial condition of the family. There should be a budget that is followed and no major purchases made without prior agreement.

That's the ideal situation. Unfortunately, most blended families are not starting off with the best of circumstances. Since this is a pre-marital guide, you should do all you can to know the financial condition of your intended spouse. It should raise a red flag to you if your intended is not forthcoming about their financial condition. Once you're married and then find out that your new spouse has thousands of dollars of debt that you didn't know about, you could find yourself responsible for half of that debt. Finding out after the fact destroys any trust that you had established with your spouse. What happens in many remarriages is that each party has a tendency to hide at least some portion of their assets until they feel they really can trust the other party. That is because they have been burned once and don't want to get burned again.

There are a few situations where separate finances (at least for a time) can facilitate having a reasonably successful blended family. If one party has been financially responsible and the other party has major debt or possibly IRS issues, it would be wise to keep things separate until the debt or tax liens can be paid off. You don't want the IRS to just come in and seize the assets of the new spouse. You can work as a team, enforcing the one-flesh relationship, pooling your assets to retire the debt. If a bankruptcy is a possibility, you will want it to only be applicable to the credit history of the spouse that incurred the debt.

Another situation that is less than ideal, but can still work if God is the center of the relationship, is where one party is very responsible but the other is not. If everything else about the relationship works for both parties, and the responsible one is willing to manage the finances and the irresponsible one is OK with just an allowance and very limited access to credit, with God's Grace, the marriage can work. With one being responsible, it can still be possible to enjoy a reasonably abundant life.

Being good stewards of what God entrusts to you is important. You would be wise to study the "Parable of the Talents" (Matthew 25:14-30; Luke 19:12-28). Making the most of what you have been given generates blessings for you, your family and God's Kingdom. If you are a poor steward, what little you have been given will be taken from you and given to someone else.

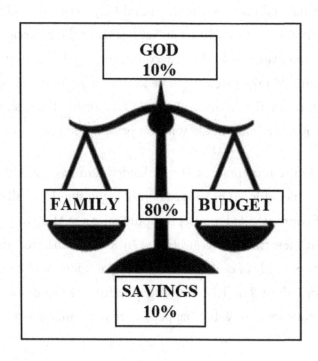

EXERCISES FOR LESSON 6

1. What is the recommended percentage breakout for your money?

2. What are your two choices if you have more month left at the end of the money?

3. Describe under what circumstances that bankruptcy might be wise. How do you reconcile that with God's word?

4. Who always gets paid first and is that before or after taxes? Who should get paid second?

CHAPTER 7

HOW TO RESOLVE CONFLICT

Conflict is not a matter of "if" but "when". As a follower of Christ, you are promised trials and tribulation. There will be times when you will be offended and you will also be the offender on occasion. How you handle the offense is directly related to your spiritual maturity. The immature often return evil for evil and react out of the emotion of the situation. The more mature Christian will take every thought captive as unto the Lord, and be more likely to respond in Grace rather than in anger after thinking things over. Anger demonstrates immaturity and a lack of understanding. Anger is one of the works of the flesh.

There are three basic reasons why God allows conflicts to come up in our lives. The first reason is to humble us. The second reason is to test our faith and the third reason is to cause us to grow spiritually. Conflict often involves the exercise of repentance, forgiveness and prayer. Since conflict is inevitable, how do you resolve a conflict with your "neighbor"?

Matthew 18:15-20 -

[15] "If your brother sins against you, go and tell him his fault, between you and him alone. If he listens to you, you have gained your brother. [16] But if he does not listen, take one or two others along with you, that every charge may be established by the evidence of two or three witnesses. [17] If he refuses to listen to them, tell it to the church. And if he refuses to listen even to the church, let him be to you as a Gentile and a tax collector. [18] Truly, I say to you, whatever you bind on earth shall be bound in heaven, and whatever you loose on earth shall be loosed in heaven. [19] Again I say to you, if two of you agree on earth about anything they ask, it will be done for them by my Father in heaven. [20] For where two or three are gathered in my name, there am I among them." (ESV).

First, you should go to the one with whom you have the conflict. State your case clearly and with personal accountability for your own feelings. Do not try to put the responsibility for your feelings on the offender. In other words, don't blame them for how you are feeling. Many offenses arise out of misunderstandings and assumptions rather than facts. Accepting responsibility for your feelings will keep the offender from feeling like they have to defend themselves from your accusation. It will create an atmosphere much more likely to result in acknowledgement of the offense by the offender and an apology to you. They you can forgive the offender and restore the relationship. If at first you don't succeed, try again with witnesses. If that doesn't work, go to the church and if that doesn't work, you are to treat them as a heathen and have nothing to do with them until such time as they are willing to repent and seek forgiveness.

Marriage, by definition is bringing two very different entities together in an attempt to create a single unit. A husband and a wife are often bringing two very different concepts of what "normal" is into the marriage. Once the honeymoon is over, this usually results in conflict. Actually, the reason the honeymoon ends is due to some sort of conflict. When conflict arises, couples should try to focus more on listening to each other than talking. When your lips are moving, it's unlikely that you are helping the situation. Be quick to listen, slow to speak and slow to anger. When you do need to speak, speak softly and use kind words.

> *James 1:19* – *Hearing and Doing the Word*
> *[19] Know this, my beloved brothers: let every person be quick to hear, slow to speak, slow to anger; (ESV)*

> *Proverbs 15:1–2*
> *[1] A soft answer turns away wrath, but a harsh word stirs up anger. [2] The tongue of the wise commends knowledge, but the mouths of fools pour out folly. (ESV)*

> *Proverbs 15:18*
> *[18] A hot-tempered man stirs up strife, but he who is slow to anger quiets contention. (ESV)*

> *Proverbs 16:23–24*
> *[23] The heart of the wise makes his speech judicious and adds persuasiveness to his lips. [24] Gracious words are like a honeycomb, sweetness to the soul and health to the body. (ESV)*

> *Proverbs 16:32*
> *[32] Whoever is slow to anger is better than the mighty, and he who rules his spirit than he who takes a city. (ESV)*

The following simple diagram illustrates the components of conflict resolution. The vertical line represents the positive or negative aspect of the affect on the marriage relationship. The horizontal line represents the positive or negative affect on the resolution of whatever the conflict is all about.

- AVOID – Mostly positive in regards to the relationship, but doesn't do anything to resolve the conflict. This eventually leads to resentment, bitterness and ultimately a big blow up after an extended period of time. This personality type hates conflict and will go to great lengths to "avoid" it. They find it very difficult to express their true feelings because they don't want to offend anyone.

- WITHDRAW – Negative on both counts. Shows a lack of ability to communicate feelings or could possibly be due to a fear of retribution. This approach does nothing positive for either the relationship or resolving a conflict. This personality type can sometimes be very manipulative, using passive aggression to get what they want by walking away in the middle of an argument. It leaves the other party in the conflict very frustrated. It's one tactic sometimes used to put a winner off balance. In an abusive relationship, it could be a matter of self-defense. Withdrawing from a conflict, or allowing the other party to win, may diffuse a conflict before it escalates to a physical abuse situation.

- WIN – Resolves the conflict for one spouse, but only at the expense of the other. If there is a "winner" there must also be a "loser". This shows a lack of concern for the other spouse's feelings, therefore it is negative in regards to the relationship. This personality type often has control issues. It's very common to see avoiders and withdrawers in relationships with winners. Winners need to be in control where the other two types are very willing to give up control to stop an argument.

- COMPROMISE – Nothing is really accomplished here other than postponing an argument. Best case is that a couple can agree to disagree agreeably. There is no victory in compromise. You see in the Old Testament that when God sent His people out to take possession of some new territory, God expected complete annihilation of the enemy – even their livestock. He did not want any trace of the enemy left behind. Without TOTAL victory, there can be no peace. Compromise is like a Peace Treaty with your enemy. Each one of you is expecting the other to violate it eventually.

- CHRIST-LIKE – This is the "What Would Jesus Do" scenario. This is where listening takes precedence over talking. Compassion for one another is held in high regard. This is where truth can be spoken in love. There is power in agreement. Make sure the Bible is the umpire for resolving conflicts. The best way to resolve conflict is to do your best to ensure each party's best interest is considered.

CONFLICT RESOLUTION DIAGRAM

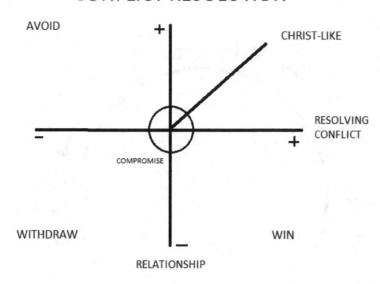

THE MARRIAGE MERRY-GO-ROUND – LOVE AND RESPECT

When there is conflict, one of the first things to happen is a couple goes for a ride on the marriage merry-go-round. The best way to start this section is with a look at Ephesians 5:21-33.

> *Ephesians 5:21–33*
>
> *[21] submitting to one another out of reverence for Christ. Wives and Husbands [22] Wives, submit to your own husbands, as to the Lord. [23] For the husband is the head of the wife even as Christ is the head of the church, his body, and is himself its Savior. [24] Now as the church submits to Christ, so also wives should submit in everything to their husbands.[25] Husbands, love your wives, as Christ loved the church and gave himself up for her, [26] that he might sanctify her, having cleansed her by the washing of water with the word, [27] so that he might present the church to himself in splendor, without spot or wrinkle or any such thing, that she might be holy and without blemish. [28] In the same way husbands should love their wives as their own bodies. He who loves his wife loves himself. [29] For no one ever hated his own flesh, but nourishes and cherishes it, just as Christ does the church, [30] because we are members of his body. [31] "Therefore a man shall leave his father and mother and hold fast to his wife, and the two shall become one flesh." [32] This mystery is profound, and I am saying that it refers to Christ and the church. [33] However, let each one of you love his wife as himself, and let the wife see that she respects her husband. (ESV)*

Every couple goes for a ride on the marriage merry-go-round sooner or later. The trick is learning how to end the ride. The following diagram illustrates how couples often operate when they are not abiding by Ephesians 5:33.

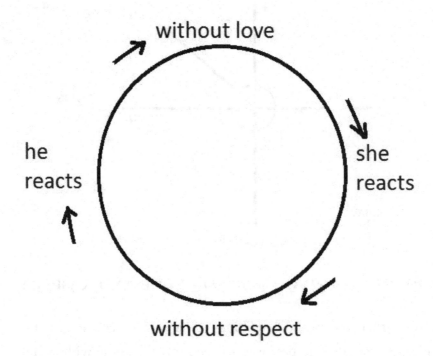

When a wife isn't feeling loved by her husband, she instinctively starts to hold back on the respect she shows to her husband. Now, when the husband starts feeling that he is not being respected, he instinctively starts withholding love he would normally show his wife. Round and round it goes. Where it stops – nobody knows. Sooner or later someone needs to wake up, figure out they are operating in the flesh and get back into the workings of the Holy Spirit.

This piece of wisdom was originally gained from a lecture given by Dr. Emerson Eggerichs. He calls this phenomenon 'The Crazy Circle'. To get more information on this subject, visit Dr. Emerson Eggerichs webite at http://www.loveandrespect.com/.

EXERCISES FOR LESSON 7

1. Looking at the Conflict Resolution Diagram, what does the "winner" actually win by forcing a conclusion to an argument?

2. When there are unresolved issues (conflicts) that you have taken the first step to deal with, what is your next step?

3. Who or what should be the umpire that has the final say for resolving conflict?

4. Describe the Marriage Merry-Go-Round.

CHAPTER 8

DISCOVER THE BLESSINGS OF BEING
CREATED DIFFERENTLY

This chapter will deal with the individual differences between the husband and the wife and the differences that come into play with the extended family. These differences include things like nationalities, cultures, races, religions, age, and geographic regions.

For this lesson, consider any marriage as the creation of a blended family. The topics discussed will apply just as much to the blending of two extended families through a first marriage as it will for the blending of two (or more) families which have step-parents involved.

As you go through life as a child, you learn your own family's traditions and their way of doing things. These things become the "normal" that you compare everything else to as you grow older. These things could be good or bad. If you feel they're good, you would want to duplicate them in your life as an adult. If you feel they were bad, they would be things that you would want to avoid doing when you're an adult and not pass them on in your own family. However, many times those bad things still get passed on in your adult life.

When God brings two people of <u>His</u> choosing together in marriage, He always brings the perfect pair of partners together that will complement each other's abilities and will help each other mature spiritually. God desires that the two, being married, will become one flesh. The goal being that the multiplication of the two parts (1 x 1 = 1) will generate something even greater than either one of the individuals standing alone. Satan will do everything he can to destroy that.

Think of magnets. Opposing magnetic forces attract and like forces repel. Would you really want to be married to someone exactly like you? Most of you would rather marry someone who would make you stronger rather than weaker. You all have various strengths and weaknesses. When you seek God and ask Him for the spouse that He has created for you, He brings to you a partner with the perfect set of complementary strengths and weaknesses. That way, as a one-flesh couple, you now have a partner that possesses strengths that offset your weaknesses. The weaknesses of the combined pair have been diminished because each partner can do things that the other isn't especially gifted in.

When you marry without seeking the Will of God first, very likely you will not have chosen the partner that God specifically created for you. You will have married for the wrong reason. In this case, it's never too late to create a new covenant and build a new relationship with God. Once each spouse turns their life over to Christ, they will begin a new journey that will bless their marriage and their families. Otherwise, they will face the consequences of failing to wait on God to provide the best mate. God always honors His covenant. You, as a sinner, often break the covenants you make, but God always keeps His. When God is brought into a marriage as the third strand of the cord, He will honor this covenant. It's not where you've been that God cares about. He cares about where you end up.

A pre-marital class such as this one really helps. It can be a real eye opener, bringing to light the really big differences two people have regarding how to handle money, how many children to have, with whose family do we celebrate holidays, how to teach and how to discipline the children. If there are any red flags, take them seriously! Make sure the red flags are all taken care of before you enter into a covenant with your intended spouse.

If you happen to already be married and now the red flags are waving like there's a hurricane coming, then you should probably call for counseling before you do anything else. Never make any major decisions when you are angry and emotionally upset. If you want to fix things <u>and</u> are willing to put in the effort to make changes from the inside out, you can achieve a great victory against the enemy that's trying to destroy you. The only person you can change in any relationship is YOU!

> <u>Proverbs 11:14</u>
> [14] *Where there is no guidance, a people falls, but in an abundance of counselors there is safety. (ESV)*

WHO'S NORMAL IS NORMAL?

Now it's time to really celebrate and discuss your differences. How do you decide who's 'normal' is right for the new blended family? As was mentioned earlier, each person's 'normal' is determined by where and the way they were brought up and the many experiences they encountered.

This is where friction often develops in a marriage. Once the honeymoon is over, the conflict between the two different 'normals' starts to become a factor in daily life. The conflicts can be over major differences as well as things that most people would consider insignificant. The Enemy likes to use your differences to create in you the feeling that one of the spouses is right (me) and the other is wrong (you). Different isn't wrong – it's just different. Differences in your pasts when looked at as something to celebrate and discover can make the journey through life together a very exciting adventure. When they are misunderstood and looked at as something to be corrected or feared, it turns life with your spouse into something to be endured rather than enjoyed.

In the majority of counseling sessions, communication is the one factor with which couples seem to have the most trouble. Communication involves a lot more listening than it does talking. You have two ears and one mouth for a reason. You need to spend time with your spouse listening to him/her describe their normal. Listen to how they feel about the way they were brought up and the many things that they experienced in their life. Listen WITHOUT JUDGMENT. The better you understand each other's normal, the better you can be at determining their needs and meeting them. Be sure to use God's Word as your base line when discussing your normals. It will help you see where changes need to be made in your own life to correct erroneous teachings from your past. Again, different isn't wrong – it's just different.

A large difference in normals can sometimes make the greatest marriage. When there is a large difference in your normals, obviously there can be some big obstacles to overcome. The bigger the gap, the greater the need for God to create the bridge that will close it. Have you ever sharpened a knife using a butcher's steel? As was stated previously:

> Proverbs 27:17
> [17] Iron sharpens iron, and one man sharpens another. (ESV)

When iron strikes iron, sometimes sparks fly. Some of the strongest and longest lasting marriages are the ones that have "good" arguments. These couples have learned the art of sharpening one another by making sparks fly once in awhile. These couples have also learned the art of forgiveness. The couples that avoid arguments look like they're OK on the surface, but underneath, their issues are never resolved and eventually something blows up and is often catastrophic.

In your day-to-day life you have many choices to make. You have to choose things such as where to live and what kind of housing, where and how you worship God, transportation options, and choices for your children's food, clothing, music and friends. Agreement between spouses when making these choices creates a powerful environment of teamwork.

Now that you've blended two families into a new one, start making your own new memories for you and all of your children. Create some brand new traditions of your own so they will have something of their own to pass onto their children. Do what you can to distinguish your blended family from either of the previous families. In the effort to create a new family with new traditions, it's important to not speak evil of the ex-spouse when there's been a divorce. It's also inappropriate to speak evil of other extended family members (in-laws). Nothing should be coming out of your mouth that doesn't edify the one you are speaking of.

> *Ephesians 4:29–32*
> *[29] Let no corrupting talk come out of your mouths, but only such as is good for building up, as fits the occasion, that it may give grace to those who hear. [30] And do not grieve the Holy Spirit of God, by whom you were sealed for the day of redemption. [31] Let all bitterness and wrath and anger and clamor and slander be put away from you, along with all malice. [32] Be kind to one another, tenderhearted, forgiving one another, as God in Christ forgave you. (ESV)*

Many have vowed at one time or another that they would never become like their parents only to catch themselves quoting what they heard as a child. Blending a family can benefit greatly from communicating about our childhood "normals" in order to make new agreed upon guidelines for discipline. For example your spouse's childhood was too strict or abusive with excessive punishment while yours was too lenient with very little discipline. In this situation, neither normal would make an appropriate role model. Search God's Word to find the right combination for dispensing grace, mercy, discipline and punishment. Pray with each other about this and then make your own list for your home as God leads you. The goal is to be able to reach an agreement as to how to raise Godly offspring. You will be powerless without it.

Don't let the differences tear you down. Let them make you stronger and find ways to use them to give your children a well-rounded education – teach them how and where you came from. Use times of discipline to teach your children about the ways of God. When you make mistakes, God uses them as teachable moments in your lives. You should do the same with your own children. When you have a trial, you are to take it to God together giving prayers of thanksgiving.

> *Ephesians 5:20–21*
> *[20] giving thanks always and for everything to God the Father in the name of our Lord Jesus Christ, [21] submitting to one another out of reverence for Christ. (ESV)*

Be silent and listen for what God is trying to teach you. Whatever He tells you to do regarding your situation you must do. He won't give you more than you can handle. Sometimes you feel you've gotten double portions and your plate is overflowing. Instead of complaining about that, thank God for the blessing of not having a plate that's empty. How loudly do people whine even over little things? Remind yourself you are the son or daughter of the King of Kings. Act accordingly. A big part of being able to live the abundant life Christ came to give us depends on your attitude.

IN-LAWS OR OUTLAWS?

Blending an extended family can be even more difficult than blending "yours, mine and ours". You have very little control over what your extended family does. You can avoid many problems by showing your in-laws the respect they are due. Take the time to get to know as many of them as possible so you can find something in common with them. Every family has the crazy uncle or someone that seems to be the odd-ball out there on the fringe of reality.

Blending the extended family can bring to light a lot of issues surrounding those cultural differences described at the beginning of this lesson. You will have in-laws that will want to dictate their own cultural ideals and normals into your blended family. Holidays can be big problem areas. Whose traditions are you going to observe? Who has the better food? The temptation the enemy puts on you in situations like this is that you will want to put your own family ahead of your spouse. That's why the Priority Pyramid should be followed.

Religious, racial and all sorts of prejudices surface when you start dealing with your extended family. Romans 2:11 shows us that to God, all people are the same. God doesn't love anyone more than anyone else. Blending a family works best when you share God's viewpoint. You are all His children and He loves you all unconditionally.

> *Romans 2:11*
> *[11] For God shows no partiality. (ESV)*

There will be many opportunities to be offended by or be offensive to your in-laws. In extreme cases of offense by in-laws, it may be necessary to set boundaries with them. Remember, the marital relationship between you and your spouse needs to be elevated above the relationship with your in-laws. Even the parent/child relationship needs to be a higher priority than the relationship with the in-laws. Being able to deal with offense is a key ingredient to a successful relationship with your in-laws. It's also a key ingredient for a successful relationship with your spouse and your children.

Offenses that occur can be related to what happens in our legal system. If you commit an offense, you can be held responsible for your actions. The person who was offended by you has the legal right to be compensated for any damages that you may have caused. Likewise, you have a legal right to seek damages from someone that offends you.

What God expects from you is to give up your right to be offended and instead, forgive the party that committed the offense. Christ gave up His right to be offended while He was being crucified and prayed, "Father, forgive them, for they know not what they do."

> *Luke 23:34*
> *[34] And Jesus said, "Father, forgive them, for they know not what they do." And they cast lots to divide his garments. (ESV)*

It's not easy, but understand that when people offend you, many times they don't even realize that they are doing it. In some cases, it's deliberate, but either way, you are still to forgive those that trespass against you.

> *Matthew 6:14-15 –*
> *[14] For if you forgive others their trespasses, your heavenly Father will also forgive you,*
> *[15] but if you do not forgive others their trespasses, neither will your Father forgive your trespasses. (ESV)*

You must forgive if you expect to be forgiven. Be quick to say, "I'm sorry." Make the effort to create a peaceful environment at home with your spouse and when you are with your in-laws. Treating your spouse with respect will return you a harvest of respect from them. As a Christian, you are called not only to be a peace keeper, but to be a peace maker.

> *James 3:18*
> *[18] And a harvest of righteousness is sown in peace by those who make peace. (ESV)*

EXERCISES FOR LESSON 8

1. Lack of _____ is the most common issue with couples that are struggling in their marriages today.

2. You have two _____ and one _____ for a reason. Explain how that affects the way you communicate.

3. Is it ever OK to speak badly about your ex-spouse or ex-in-laws?

4. Describe what kind of attitude God wants us to have towards others who offend us and why.

CHAPTER 9

SPECIAL SITUATIONS AFFECTING BLENDED FAMILIES

With blended families, there are so many variables that come into play as you are getting ready to remarry. Red flags can pop up over things that would be just a normal part of life for a family that has been intact for several generations. There will be many challenges to face when you start forging relationships with the people your new spouse has known all their life. There is an expectation that the "new guy" in the relationship will feel the same about your relatives as you do. If that doesn't work out, you will have an area of conflict to deal with.

BECOMING A STEP-CHILD AS AN ADULT

Many remarriages are taking place with individuals that are getting older. More and more mature marriages are ending in divorce after 20, 30 and even 40+ years of marriage. Something that is happening frequently today is that children that grew up in a very functional, loving "normal" home with their biological parents are finding that they are now adult step-children when one of their parents gets remarried.

The old normal for remarriage was due to the death of a spouse. Today it is just as likely to be from divorce and both of your parents are still alive. Now you will have to go through many of the emotions that younger kids experience when the 10-year or less marriage ends in divorce. Hopefully, though, by now you will be more mature in your Christian walk and be able to forgive your parents and still love both of them even though they don't love each other right now. You will need to be aware that as a step-child, you will be exposed to a whole new set of step-relatives. Some of them may turn out to be a real blessing to you and others may not.

If you are going to be entering into a blended family situation, be prepared to work with your new kids. If you happen to be in that group of people where you became a step-child as an adult, you should be able to relate better to how the younger child feels about you being their step-parent. If you have never been a parent and are now faced with the fact that you will soon become a step-parent, implementing the "Golden Rule" found in Matthew 7:12 and Luke 6:31 will help you work through some of the situations that you will face.

WORKING WITH YOUR NEW STEP-CHILDREN

Dealing with the emotional trauma suffered by the children after a divorce or even the death of a parent is another area in which blended families are challenged. Many times, after a divorce, the children end up feeling guilt believing that they were somehow responsible for the divorce. They might feel shame now that their parents have split up. After divorce, the children have lots of emotions that, depending on their maturity, they may not know how to deal with. Sometimes you are blessed and the children adapt amazingly well as God's gift of resiliency shines through them. Perhaps that is due to their biological parents' intentional efforts. Others are often angry at one or both of their parents and take it out on everyone they meet. They have lost much of the security that kids require in life. If they have lost one or both of their parents to an accident or illness, they will often feel like they have been abandoned. Again, it takes a special person with a lot of love, compassion and patience to willingly step into a blended situation where there are children who are angry or deliberately uncooperative. You can not enter into a situation like this expecting your new spouse to automatically put you ahead of their children. Getting the Priority Pyramid in place requires much time, effort, patience and prayer. It doesn't happen overnight.

CARE-GIVERS FOR ELDERLY FAMILY MEMBERS

Today, future in-laws are living longer than ever. What happens, for example, if you've fallen in love with someone that has been the primary care giver for an elderly family member? This particular situation can also make it difficult to implement God's Priority Pyramid successfully in the very beginning. It should still be a goal, but it will take patience and time to incorporate and may even include educating the elderly family member about the new marital relationship.

It takes a very special person to marry someone knowing that there will be many times when you will have to take second place to the elderly family member's needs. If a person has the right (Holy) spirit, they should be able to handle this type of situation because they understand that a marriage should be about serving your spouse. You are not promised that you will have tomorrow. In this case, are you willing to get married today knowing it may be a matter of years before you are able to have your spouse to yourself? You will be competing with a prior commitment made to that family member ensuring they will be taken care of. You can not expect your future spouse to quit on that commitment. You will be marrying your spouse and at least for a time, their family member. As with your other major decisions, definitely pray about it first and take time to hear from God.

WHO GETS TO KEEP THE FRIENDS?

Something that should be considered, but which is much less significant than other matters discussed here is who gets to keep the friends after a divorce. If you are about to remarry, you need to find out who you future spouse's friends are. Hopefully, you'll get to meet them before you get married and they will give you their stamp of approval. If, for some reason they do not approve of you, that can be a huge red flag. Friends of your intended spouse will undoubtedly have some influence over them. If for some reason they do not approve of you, they will be doing their best to keep you from getting married.

This is also an area difficult to move into proper priority since these relationships existed prior to your entrance. Lack of understanding as to the proper order of relationships often results in conflict in a remarriage. Instead of putting the relationships in God's order, the tendency is to put your relationships in order by seniority. Relationships you've had with friends the longest end up being given the most value. That conflicts with the order in the Priority Pyramid. Your new spouse often ends up taking a back seat compared to the friends that you've had for many years. That inevitably results in resentment and bitterness in the new spouse. Remember, a husband and wife are to become one flesh.

Divorce can create some rather unusual alliances. When there has been a divorce and the divorced couple had other "couple" friends, which divorced spouse gets to keep the friends? Couples frequently shy away from couples they used to hang out with once they get divorced. One reason is that it is just awkward. If you liked both parties before the divorce, how can you still like both of them when they usually hate each other and are tearing each other down? Another reason married couples keep divorced friends at a distance is that now that the divorced parties are "available', it can be seen as a potential threat to the couple that is still married.

WHO GETS TO KEEP THE PETS

Pets can occasionally create situations that need to be worked out before getting married. If one of you is a dog lover and the other is a cat lover, you may want to agree on not having pets at all. If you are about to remarry someone that kept the family pet after a divorce, you had better be ready to "adopt" the pet. Usually it is not a big problem, but in some cases, the pet will not adopt you and that will generally be where the problem occurs. If your intended spouse has had the pet to themselves for an extended amount of time, it is very likely they treat the pet as their child.

Any discussion about getting rid of the pet would be like asking them to get rid of one of their kids. The Priority Pyramid diagram doesn't address the pet relationship, but if it did, the pets would be on the bottom. Relationships with family, friends and other people should be more important than your relationship with an animal. God created us to have dominion over the plants and animals. They are not on the same level as humans. Before the wedding, make sure any issues with existing pets are resolved to the satisfaction of both parties. You don't want to end up in the position of having to make a choice between a spouse and a pet.

Remarriage is nothing like getting married for the first time. You not only have your own baggage to carry around and deal with, now you have at least some of the baggage left over from someone else's life. This is why it is so important for a soon-to-be blended family to receive pre-marital counseling. Too many times, people get married blindly, expecting things to just work themselves out on their own. Later, when you start experiencing the challenges, you can be caught off guard and be unprepared to deal with the more difficult ones. That is why the divorce rate among remarried couples is much higher and quicker than first marriages. Two people that feel they are ready to become a new blended family need to be aware of these types of things. And simply going through motions of attending pre-marital counseling without completing the 'homework' will not help resolve existing issues and situations.

EXERCISES FOR LESSON 9

1. Explain how you would handle inheriting a 40-something step-son or step-daughter in your new blended family. What if they were facing a major crisis in their own life?

2. Should your spouse get to keep the previous family's pet? What should you do if the pet doesn't like you? Where do pets fit in according to the Priority Pyramid?

3. How can you implement the Priority Pyramid when your future spouse's parents are going to have to live with you?

4. Do you know what your future spouse's favorite meal is? Describe how you would go about preparing and serving it to them to make it a very special occasion.

CHAPTER 10

TAKE TIME TO HEAL

Before you jump into a remarriage with all the challenges that await you, take time to heal. Whether it is from a divorce or the actual death of a spouse, you have suffered a great loss. It is especially important to allow the children affected by the divorce a chance to deal with their feelings. Give the children time to heal and adjust to their new situation before you start a new relationship. It will save you many hours of grief later because if you don't, you will be forcing the children to adapt to a situation they really aren't emotionally prepared for.

God's timing is perfect. If you find yourself forcing things to happen to suit your own purposes, it most likely is not the time that God would have you doing those things. After a divorce, you really need to grieve the death of that marriage just as if you were grieving the loss of any other loved one. When you don't take the time to grieve, you end up carrying those feelings into the next relationship. If you haven't honestly dealt with your feelings about the former relationship and the former spouse, you will end up bringing unforgiveness into the new relationship. Unforgiveness is a sin. When you bring sin into a new relationship, you are bringing poison from the old into the new. If the poison doesn't end up killing the new relationship, it will never be a truly healthy one unless/until the poison is removed through awareness and healing.

To have the best chance at survival 'till death do us part", a marriage needs to have both parties individually enter whole. God multiplies and adds. One of His favorite equations is "1 times 1 = 1". In order for that equation to come out right, the husband and wife need to be whole "ones". If either of you is not whole, when you are multiplied together, the result is less than 1. When you start multiplying fractions, the pieces of the pie keep getting smaller. The enemy divides and subtracts. If you're not sure where those little voices in your head are coming from, do the math.

A big challenge for a blended family is that one or both parties about to be married have not truly healed from the loss of the previous marriage. There is significant baggage that is being carried by each one. Forgiveness is a first step towards releasing all the baggage that you took with you from the previous relationship.

Getting to know yourself from God's viewpoint is a good first step in understanding why you need to be forgiven as well as willing to forgive. Being able to look into a mirror and see what God sees will enable you to start walking down the path of change. You'll be able to start changing your behavior. Your general outlook on life will improve and the way you interact with others will bless them and you as well. The happiest people are those that have an attitude of gratitude. Through increased knowledge and understanding of what God truly says about you, the healing of old wounds can begin. There is freedom to be gained by believing God. There is bondage to be suffered by believing the lies of the Devil. The following explains the importance of forgiveness.

WHY FORGIVE?

When you've committed a sin, it's a sin against God not just another person. You have just put a roadblock in the vertical relationship between you and God. The process of dealing with sin consists of being convicted by the Holy Spirit which produces a Godly sorrow for the sin. Godly sorrow is a deep recognition and understanding that you have done something to offend God. That's different than the superficial sorrow you feel when you get caught doing something wrong. You have to confess the sin to God with a sincere heartfelt attitude of repentance. God will then be faithful to forgive your sins. God forgives and makes a point to erase it from His memory. To Him, it's like it never happened. For man, it's harder to forget, but with true forgiveness, the pain will fade.

> *Psalms 103:8-12*
> *[8] The LORD is merciful and gracious, slow to anger and abounding in steadfast love. [9] He will not always chide, nor will he keep his anger forever. [10] He does not deal with us according to our sins, nor repay us according to our iniquities. [11] For as high as the heavens are above the earth, so great is his steadfast love toward those who fear him; [12] as far as the east is from the west, so far does he remove our transgressions from us. (ESV)*

Most people have an easier time asking God to forgive them when it's just between them and God. It's more difficult for people to let go of things that someone else did to them. Offense is an interesting trap. When you are offended, you want to blame the offending party for "making" you feel angry or hurt. That would be fine if the other party actually had the power to do that. It's your emotion, you either control it, or it will control you. Emotion causes you to <u>react</u> based on how you feel without considering all the facts. When you are the Master of your emotions, you consider the situation fully and then <u>respond</u> based on what you know to be true.

Your normal reaction to an offense is to get even. Scripture clearly tells us that vengeance is only for the Lord to handle. Only in His control can perfect justice be applied to those who offend His children. In our humanness, we are not privy to the ultimate Will of God. That's why we need to take every thought captive, put our 'God Glasses' on and respond as Jesus would.

> *Romans 12:19*
> *[19] Beloved, never avenge yourselves, but leave it to the wrath of God, for it is written,*
> *"Vengeance is mine, I will repay, says the Lord." (ESV)*

When you encounter a situation that creates an offense against you, the Enemy now has an open door to inflict more pain and suffering. Every offense against you, when not forgiven, becomes like another brick in your backpack. An offense to you should be seen as an object that's laid at your feet. You have to make a conscious decision to either pick it up and carry it with you or just let it lay there. If you pick it up, it becomes your possession and now you own it. You are responsible for it. If you don't pick it up, you don't have to carry it around with you or make room in your daily life for it to continue to exist.

It's also something you have the option to remove from your backpack at any time to lighten your load. Adding the brick to your backpack is the same as you committing a sin in the earlier paragraph. Before you choose to feel offended, remember what Christ said on the cross in Luke 23:34. Forgiveness removes the brick from the backpack and restores the vertical relationship with God and then He can start the process of healing your wound.

> <u>*Luke 23:34*</u>
> *[34] And Jesus said, "Father, forgive them, for they know not what they do." And they*
> *cast lots to divide his garments. (ESV)*

Forgiveness is something you do for yourself. It's not something you do for the person that committed the offense against you. Forgiving others is a prerequisite for having your own sins forgiven. As Matthew 6 states, you will be forgiven according to the same measure you forgive others and if you do not forgive, you will not be forgiven.

Matthew 6:12 -

[12] and forgive us our debts, as we also have forgiven our debtors. (ESV)

Matthew 6:14–15

[14] For if you forgive others their trespasses, your heavenly Father will also forgive you, [15] but if you do not forgive others their trespasses, neither will your Father forgive your trespasses. (ESV)

Later in the book of Matthew, Jesus teaches us that there is no limit to the amount of forgiving that we must do and reinforces the fact that God will not forgive us if we do not forgive.

Matthew 18:21–35 The Parable of the Unforgiving Servant

[21] Then Peter came up and said to him, "Lord, how often will my brother sin against me, and I forgive him? As many as seven times?" [22] Jesus said to him, "I do not say to you seven times, but seventy-seven times. [23] "Therefore the kingdom of heaven may be compared to a king who wished to settle accounts with his servants. [24] When he began to settle, one was brought to him who owed him ten thousand talents. [25] And since he could not pay, his master ordered him to be sold, with his wife and children and all that he had, and payment to be made. [26] So the servant fell on his knees, imploring him, 'Have patience with me, and I will pay you everything.' [27] And out of pity for him, the master of that servant released him and forgave him the debt. [28] But when that same servant went out, he found one of his fellow servants who owed him a hundred denarii, and seizing him, he began to choke him, saying, 'Pay what you owe.' [29] So his fellow servant fell down and pleaded with him, 'Have patience with me, and I will pay you.' [30] He refused and went and put him in prison until he should pay the debt. [31] When his fellow servants saw what had taken place, they were greatly distressed, and they went and reported to their master all that had taken place. [32] Then his master summoned him and said to him, 'You wicked servant! I forgave you all that debt because you pleaded with me. [33] And should not you have had mercy on your fellow servant, as I had mercy on you?' [34] And in anger his master delivered him to the jailers, until he should pay all his debt. [35] So also my heavenly Father will do to every one of you, if you do not forgive your brother from your heart." (ESV)

In the era of Grace and Mercy brought to you through Jesus Christ, you have been given freedom from the laws that applied in the Old Testament (see Galatians 5:13-15). Love fulfills the law. However, God's principles still apply. The gift of salvation is Grace in action. Mercy keeps you from getting stoned (with rocks) every time you do something wrong. In simple terms, Grace is getting what you don't deserve and Mercy is NOT getting what you DO deserve.

Galatians 5:13–15

[13] For you were called to freedom, brothers. Only do not use your freedom as an opportunity for the flesh, but through love serve one another. [14] For the whole law is fulfilled in one word: "You shall love your neighbor as yourself." [15] But if you bite and devour one another, watch out that you are not consumed by one another. (ESV)

Understanding the truth, that through repentance and forgiveness you are set free from the bondage of sin, can transform a marriage. It is very wise for you to really spend some time prior to getting married to seek forgiveness from God and to forgive yourself from the sins of the past. Doing this allows you to start fresh with much fewer chances of hitting unseen potholes on your new road through life together.

EXERCISES FOR LESSON 10

1. When you commit a sin against someone, who else is it committed against? Who takes ownership of sin? The person committing it or the person that it is committed against? Explain.

2. What happens when you don't forgive an offense? "You have just added a _____ to your _____."

3. Who benefits most from forgiveness? You or the offender? _____

4. Math quiz – what is ½ times ½? _____ Describe why each party about to be married should be healed and whole before they are actually married.

CHAPTER 11

BEFORE YOU SAY "I DO"

Before you actually say, "I do." make sure you have taken a really good look in the mirror and have laid your issues at the foot of the cross. This curriculum has attempted to take you on a journey to open your eyes to the many benefits and blessings as well as the challenges of creating a new family from pieces. You either have the pieces that remain from a family that suffered the loss of a parent or one that suffered defeat by the enemy doing battle in spiritual warfare. The wisdom gleaned from the scriptures and practical knowledge gained from over 30 years of experience living as a blended family has been poured into this teaching. You can do it your way and make all the same mistakes, otherwise known as "experience", or exercise "wisdom" and learn from someone else's mistakes. It's your choice.

God is a God of do-overs. Make every attempt to become a new creation in Christ. Jesus paid the price for ALL sins. There is no more debt to be paid. There are still consequences, but the debt (death) has been paid in full. The enemy would have you be chained to your past. He will constantly remind you that you have committed sins of various kinds. He will tempt you, he will accuse you of your past and he will try to intimidate you with your mistakes from the past. Understand you can not undo what you have done. However, today is a new day. Yes, but today really is the first day of the rest of your life. You can start today to become that new creation as described in 2nd Corinthians 5:16-21. Pay close attention to verse 17.

> Look at 2 Corinthians 5:16-21 -
>
> *[16] From now on, therefore, we regard no one according to the flesh. Even though we once regarded Christ according to the flesh, we regard him thus no longer. [17] Therefore, if anyone is in Christ, he is a new creation. The old has passed away; behold, the new has come. [18] All this is from God, who through Christ reconciled us to himself and gave us the ministry of reconciliation; [19] that is, in Christ God was reconciling the world to himself, not counting their trespasses against them, and entrusting to us the message of reconciliation. [20] Therefore, we are ambassadors for Christ, God making his appeal through us. We implore you on behalf of Christ, be reconciled to God. [21] For our sake he made him to be sin who knew no sin, so that in him we might become the righteousness of God. (ESV)*

This particular piece of Scripture has immense healing power when it is received into your spirit. Since there are many divorces that result from all sorts of addictive behaviors, make sure that your future spouse has taken the appropriate steps to be delivered from those addictions and has truly given their life to Christ. You do not want to be unequally yoked because you will definitely be fighting an uphill battle. Especially in a blended family where you are starting over after what is often a very traumatic experience, it benefits you greatly to be able to start with a clean sheet of paper. The more scribbling there is on your paper, the harder it is to write a new chapter in your life.

God said it was not good for man to be alone. Marriage is something created and ordained by God to fulfill the need in a man and a woman to have a relationship. He expects you to have a relationship with Him on a spiritual level but He also expects you to have a loving relationship with someone that you can spend you whole life with. Before you say, "I do." make sure you are mentally and emotionally ready and you have a new palette and a new canvas to create your new tapestry for the rest of your life.

In Proverbs 18:22 it is written that *[22] He who finds a wife finds a good thing and obtains favor from the LORD. (ESV)* Marriage is what God intended for Man to use to take dominion over the Earth. It is very near and dear to the heart of God. God, being love, is all about relationships. He desires that everyone would have a relationship with Him and as Jesus commanded, "Love thy neighbor as thyself." Do you see where you need to love yourself first (as a child of God, loved unconditionally) before you can love someone else? You can't give what you don't have. You are to have a spiritual, physical and emotional relationship with God as well as your spouse.

Look at your upcoming wedding as an opportunity to start over. Yes, there will be many challenges as you have seen throughout the previous chapters. If you know they are coming, you can be prepared for them and meet them head-on and get through them with Christ at your side. It's those things that you are not prepared for that may defeat you. Put Christ at the head of your marriage and when you and your soon-to-be spouse are both in submission to Him first and then to one another you will be very blessed. As soon as you start looking at what you are getting out of the relationship, your focus will be on what your spouse is doing wrong or what they aren't doing to meet your needs.

Selfishness is the beginning of division. It's no longer about "us", it's now all about "me". In many weddings, part of the ceremony involves the use of the "unity" candle. Each party has their own candle and then they come together and light the unity candle. Once the unity candle has been lit, each party blows out their own personal candle. This is a great representation as to what marriage is all about. You no longer are just you; you are now part of something larger than yourself. Now, you have to keep working at not re-lighting your own candle. Marriage is about serving one another as Christ came to serve rather than being served.

By now, any potential red flags should be flying prominently. Please do not get married until you have addressed each and every red flag. Those red flags represent the conviction of the Holy Spirit that something is wrong. Whatever might be wrong needs to be openly dealt with before the new covenant begins. That red flag might just be what saves you from a life of misery. Have you and your intended thoroughly discussed everything? Have you talked about sex? If there had ever been any sort of abuse in your past, have you forgiven the offender? Past sexual abuse can create problems in your new relationship if you have tried to simply hide it and have not fully resolved the issues from the emotional trauma suffered in the past.

Have you discussed such things as medical conditions? If you happen to suffer from some condition that may shorten your expected life, have you let your intended spouse know about it? Do you have something like HIV that could be transmitted to your partner? Are there any unusual genetic issues that your future spouse may need to know about should you choose to have more children together? These are all things that can be dealt with if you know about them ahead of time. Love can overcome all sorts of inconveniences, trials and tribulations. If you enter into a relationship with true love, honesty, respect and with the power of the Holy Spirit, you can make it something beautiful.

Are you still young enough to consider having children with your new spouse? Have you discussed that with them? How many would you want to have? Make sure you follow the Priority Pyramid and if either of you are bringing children from a previous marriage, make sure you treat all the children involved as "ours". Do not make the mistake of trying to maintain the distinction of "yours", "mine" and "ours".

Since you should each have your own residence and haven't been cohabitating before the wedding, have you discussed what you are going to do about choosing a place to live? If you are currently cohabitating and are engaging in pre-marital sex, you are committing the sin of fornication. It can be forgiven, but it needs to stop now! Cleansing yourself from this unrighteousness is covered in Chapter 12.

Are you already in the same city? Will one of you have to relocate to a different part of the country or even a different country altogether? What are you going to do for employment if you are the one that has to relocate? What will your spouse do while you're looking for a new job? Can you afford to live on only one of your incomes? What is going to be considered "junk" once you combine all your stuff into one household? Who gets to decide what gets thrown away and what stays? Have you talked about your driving record? Is it squeaky clean or do you have a tendency to get speeding tickets? Bad credit, poor driving records and felony convictions are all things that make for unappreciated surprises. These things tend to follow you for a long time and can be difficult to overcome – especially when you need to find a new job. Before you say, "I do" make sure you know who you are about to marry.

Have you discussed your ideas about how the children should be disciplined? Are you going to follow the Godly standard or do you want to take care of "your" kids and let your spouse take care of "their" kids? Remember from before, there is power in agreement. Agreement is vital when it comes to the discipline of the children. You may win a few battles, but you will ultimately lose the war if you and your spouse are not in agreement about discipline in the home.

One possible red flag area that has not been discussed in much detail so far is that of motives. Do you believe your intended spouse really loves you with a Godly love, or is it possible they want to make sure no one else gets you? Are there issues with jealousy and control? Do they tell you how to do even the smallest things? Do they threaten you with leaving the relationship or worse, like physical harm? Are you the one that has these issues? Better to avoid situations like that because they can be very difficult to get out of later. The party that has issues in this area is not going to want to change because of pride. They won't see themselves as having a problem or needing to change their behavior.

Before you say, "I do", consider discussing some of the longer term issues of life. Talk about wills, medical powers of attorney, living wills, DNR (do not resuscitate) orders, wills and estate planning. Do either of you have an estate large enough that you should consider forming a trust once you are married? Do either of you have life insurance? Do you plan to get some once you are married? Discuss how you are going to set up the beneficiaries. You should each be each other's primary, but since you will be a blended family, there are other scenarios that need to be considered. How old are the children involved? Are they already adults with their own families? Do you need to provide for a college education or living expenses for a young child should you be called up by the Lord before you thought you would be? Once you are a blended family, you need to have legal plans for the step-parent to be the official guardian (if that is your agreement) should something happen to the birth parent. The potential exists for ex-spouses or even ex-grandparents to file suit against the remaining step-parent to gain custody of their children or grandchildren if the birth mother or father is no longer living.

Be aware that in many cases of divorce, your ex-spouse might have had a pretty good relationship with your parents. It was just you he/she couldn't get along with. This presents another situation that can be very difficult to deal with in a new blended family. For example, if your ex-wife and your mother really had a close relationship before the divorce, you can't really expect your mother to all of a sudden dispose of that relationship and act like it never happened. You will need to lovingly educate your mother that she needs to respect your new spouse and that there needs to be boundaries when it relates to your ex. You no longer have a relationship with the ex.

The ex may have custody of your child and your mother obviously needs to see her grandchild and continue to build relationship. The mother needs to understand that continuing a "close" relationship with the ex is interfering with your new marriage. The mother will need to put some distance between your ex and herself. They should still be Christ-like to each other, but there should be very limited discussion as to what you and your new spouse are doing. In some cases, the ex will try to maintain the relationship with your mother out of spite, other times they really are a decent human being and it's you that messed things up. This is one of those situations that many blended families find themselves having to deal with. You are not alone in this.

EXERCISES FOR LESSON 11

1. Discuss the importance of being a new creation in Christ before you are about to remarry.

2. Why do so many people remarry? With what need did God create us?

3. _____ is the beginning of division. Explain why?

4. Explain how you would handle a situation where your mother still maintains a close relationship with your ex-spouse. How does Matthew 5:43-44 apply to this situation?

CHAPTER 12

YOUR COVENANT MARRIAGE

If you haven't been totally frightened away from becoming a blended family by now, you should be well prepared to proceed with the wedding. You and your intended spouse should know each other very well. You should have reasonable expectations about what types of things could happen. You should understand that it really does take a special type of person to step into a blended family and work with someone else's children and create new relationships with a different extended family. You know now that you could be in for a real roller coaster ride through life by taking on the role of step-parent.

What is a covenant marriage? About.com defines it as follows: "A covenant marriage is a form of marriage that makes it more difficult to divorce. In the United States covenant marriages are an option for couples in Arizona, Arkansas, and Louisiana. Couples in those three states can decide when they apply for a marriage license to have a covenant marriage or they can wait until after they are married to upgrade their marriage to a covenant marriage. Generally, when a couple decides to have a covenant marriage, they must attend premarital counseling before getting married. If their marriage is in trouble and they want to divorce, they have to seek counseling and wait for a longer period before a divorce is granted."

An old adage says, "Once burned, twice shy". When it comes to marriage, that old adage is often true as well. Something happening more and more today is the use of pre-nuptial contracts. This flies in the face of covenant marriage because it treats marriage simply as a business deal. It's all about the money. It has nothing to do with God's plan or marriage being a covenant. The expectation is set in the beginning that the marriage is eventually going to fail. Without a covenant mentality, you don't have the understanding of what God intended marriage to be from the beginning. Without a covenant mentality and an eternal focus, you won't be able to withstand the trials and tribulations that will come against you from time to time. With an eternal perspective, you can see that the various trials and tribulations are just a temporary condition and that God will see you through.

A covenant marriage requires intentional and committed effort on each spouse's part. You are not going to succeed if you try to "get by" with half-hearted effort. Whenever God made a covenant with Man, it was always sealed with a blood sacrifice. A blood covenant with God was only broken when the person that made the covenant with God died. God would honor His end of that covenant as long as that person was alive. A marriage is a blood covenant. God intended that a husband and wife would enter into a marriage as virgins. On the wedding night, if the wife was a virgin, there would be a small issue of blood when her hymen was broken. Medical research has yet to find any functional reason for a hymen. God put it there so that when a husband and a wife had made a vow to each other in His presence and then consummated the marriage, that covenant would be sealed with blood.

It's extremely unlikely that two people getting remarried would ever still be virgins. If one of you has never been married before, then it would be possible, but in today's world, still rather unlikely. Praise the Lord if you have remained a virgin until marriage. So how do you enter into your new marriage with the full blessings that God intended for first-time marriages? First thing – stop cohabitating!

> _Galatians 5:19_
> _[19] Now the works of the flesh are evident: sexual immorality, impurity, sensuality,_
> _(ESV)_

> _Ephesians 5:3_
> _[3] But sexual immorality and all impurity or covetousness must not even be named among you, as is proper among saints. (ESV)_

Repent of your sins and seek forgiveness from the Lord. Spend some time apart, abstaining from sex between now and the wedding. Dedicate yourselves and your new marriage to God. You can be spiritually cleansed and restored to that virgin state. After the wedding, enter into the new blood covenant between you and your spouse in the presence of God through the consummation of your marriage.

When both parties in a marriage have that eternal covenant outlook, it creates a sense of security. Security allows for the freedom to speak openly about things without fear of someone wanting to leave the relationship. With a long-term outlook, crisis becomes an opportunity to get closer to your spouse and, with God's Grace, you can make it through the crisis even stronger than when it first arose. The Chinese have an interesting way of looking at crisis. Their symbol for the word "crisis" consists of the symbol for "danger" and the symbol for "opportunity".

Often, the "danger" part of the equation is there to get our attention. It puts us in a place where we may not survive on our own and we need God. God allows crisis in our lives to give us opportunities to grow and mature spiritually. If you can grasp the idea that trials and tribulations are often tests being allowed by God, you can follow the thinking that each test is an open-book test (Bible) and the teacher (Christ) is always available to help you take the test. You don't have to take the test all alone. The tests are Pass/Fail so once you pass, you can move on to another test. If you fail, you will have to keep taking the test again and again until you finally "get it" and pass the test.

The covenant that a husband and a wife enter into when they are married represents the covenant Christ has with His bride – the Church. In Old Testament days, the Hebrew wedding feast was symbolic of this future wedding between Christ and His Church. The Groom-to-be stood at one end of the banquet table and the Bride-to-be was seated at the opposite end. The Groom's family was seated on one side of the table and the Bride's family on the other. The Groom would take a loaf of bread, break off a piece and pass it down the Bride's side of the table. The bread symbolized the Groom's promise to provide for his Bride. Each member of the Bride's family would break off a piece of bread and eat it and then pass it down. If anyone of the Bride's family did not approve, they held the loaf of bread without eating. Then, the Groom would take a sip from a cup of wine and pass it down his family's side of the table. The wine symbolized the Groom's continuation of his family's bloodline. Through the children she would bear, the Groom's family would continue for generations. Any children they would have together would carry the Groom's family name. If any one of the Groom's family did not approve of the Bride, they would stop the passing of the cup. If everyone approved, the Bride would have received the bread (promise of provision) and the cup of wine (bloodline). She ate of the bread and sipped from the cup to seal the acceptance of the proposal. Today, we celebrate this through the taking of Communion – remembering Christ through the eating of bread and drinking of 'fruit of the vine'.

Please hear these final words about your upcoming covenant marriage. The Bible needs to be your 'go-to' marriage reference manual. When you and your intended have difficulty agreeing about any questions you may have, please refer to the Holy Scriptures for the final answer. Scripture is the absolute truth. It is not opinion. Dig deep for the wisdom that is to be found there. When you two have 'opinions' that don't match, it's possible that you could both be wrong. Do not waste your time arguing over who's right and who's wrong. Two different answers can never both be correct, but they can both be wrong. Go to the Bible and get the truth. Many arguments amount to each individual wanting to be right in their own thinking. Many times, both perspectives are basically the same, but the parties are using different words to communicate their ideas.

Take time to be with God every day reading His Word and in prayer. Be intentional about your vertical relationship with Him so that your horizontal one with your spouse will be blessed. Keep that covenant mentality and practice unconditional love. You are receiving it from God every day. You are both expected to be submissive to each other, being servants. He expects you to pass it on – especially to your covenant partner for life. If you ever have trouble finding something to talk about, you can always talk about what God is doing in your life. Share your praise reports. It gives others hope and helps you through the tough times. Pray to receive the vision for your blended family that God has prepared just for you. Many people will tell you, "Life is what YOU make it." An abundant life is a life lived through Christ. God is your provider, place of refuge and tower of strength. Don't pray for opportunities; instead, pray that you will be ready for them when they come. Open your heart and mind to receive the blessings that God has prepared for you. You should now be ready to tackle the many challenges of a blended family. With the right attitude and a focus on God, you will find that the blessings will far outnumber the challenges. May God truly bless you and your new blended family.

EXERCISES FOR LESSON 12

Now that you have reached the end of this book, it would be a good time to reflect on what you have learned and write your vision statement for your new marriage. First, take some time to pray over and about your plans. Where do you see your marriage going in the years to come? Once you have received and written your vision statement, document your plan to accomplish that vision. Write out your goals. Create your road map here. First write your individual goals and then work together to blend 'your' goals into 'our' goals. May God bless you and keep you and may you abide in Him. In Jesus' Name. Amen.

ABOUT THE AUTHORS

Dr. Larry and Dr. Carol Snapp were married from December, 1979 until Dr. Carol's passing in April of 2024. When they got married, they created a blended family. Carol had been married twice before and had step children. She knows what the term, 'Yours, Mine and Ours' means. Larry had never married before. Larry inherited 3 children that Carol had from her previous 2 marriages.

After 23 years of marriage, they experienced a major crisis. Through a friend who introduced them to the NAME marriage ministry, God brought them together with an awesome Care Couple. With God's help, they were restored and after several years of counseling others struggling in their marriages, God gave them a vision for this ministry.

Through their own experience they learned many good ways and bad ways to do things. Ultimately, they learned the Godly way to do things. They had to walk through many months of trials and tribulations first hand to gain the understanding for this teaching.

Through all the testing, God put a desire in their hearts to put family values back into homes. By reaching out to one family, one man, one woman, or even one child at a time they hope to teach God's plan for marriage. As one is taught, they in turn are able to teach others in their family or their friend's family in return. Their vision is to have this spread like a virus worldwide. Instead of a virus that makes you sick, this virus will heal you, your marriage and your family.

Larry is still committed to God's work of rebuilding His image in hearts and minds – one family at a time.

Hopefully, God will touch your heart and you will be infected by this virus and join Blended Families Ministry in their work.

Printed in the United States
by Baker & Taylor Publisher Services